THE HOUSE ON HENRY STREET

PHILANTHROPY AND SOCIETY
Richard Magat, Series Editor

THE HOUSE ON HENRY STREET

Lillian D. Wald

With a New Introduction by
Eleanor L. Brilliant

With Illustrations from Etchings and Drawings
by Abraham Phillips and from Photographs

Transaction Publishers
New Brunswick (U.S.A.) and London (U.K.)

New material this edition © 1991 by Transaction Publishers, New Brunswick, New Jersey 08903. Original copyright © 1915. Originally published in 1915 by Henry Holt and Company.

Library of Congress Catalog Number: 90-40716
ISBN: 0-88738-384-X
Printed in the United States of America

Library of Congress Cataloging-in-Publication Data

Wald, Lillian D., 1867-1940
    The house on Henry Street/ Lillian D. Wald: with an introduction by
    Eleanor Brilliant
      p.   cm. -(Philanthropy and society)
    Reprint. Originally published: New York: H. Holt, 1915
    Includes index.
    ISBN 0-88738-384-X (cloth)
    1. Henry Street Settlement (New York, N.Y.) 2. Poor–New York (N.Y.)
    I.Title. II. Series.
    HV4196.N6H5   1990   90-40716
    362.5'09747'1-dc20   CIP

CONTENTS

INTRODUCTION TO THE
TRANSACTION EDITION

Nearly one hundred years after the founding of Henry Street Settlement and seventy-five years after Lillian D. Wald wrote *The House on Henry Street*, her book is being reissued in this new edition. Perhaps the best testimony to the continuing importance of its message is the vitality of the venerable institution that remains on the lower East Side of New York. Although it is serving different people, and has changed in several ways, Henry Street Settlement is still very much alive and well. Much of the credit for its continued existence may be given to the foundation provided by Lillian Wald herself, as described in her book.

In the book's concluding pages, Miss Wald comments on the steady stream of famous visitors coming to Henry Street from foreign shores.[1] She might be comforted to note that the tradition continues; in February 1989, the Princess of Wales visited the Settlement.[2] It was more than just sentiment that prompted the visit. The royal visitor would have seen the same core of houses that served the Settlement residents in Lillian Wald's day, and she observed programmatic activities similar to those that were formulated when Lillian Wald was head worker.

The House on Henry Street was written at the height of the Progressive era, when economic prosperity and an expansive spirit were pervasive in our country, but when poverty and misery were the lot of countless new immigrants and inner-city families. The book accordingly is both the story of the early years of the Henry Street Settlement and the story of the personal involvement of Lillian Wald in the social reform activities of the Settlement and the Progressive movement. As one of the earlier scholarly reviewers noted, "Miss Wald's fascinating human document gives substantial proof of the accomplishment of the Settlement in economic and social reform."[3]

The House on Henry Street initially appeared in serial form in *The Atlantic Monthly*, from March through August 1915, and apparently was not intended to be a published book. But Miss Wald was encouraged to turn it into a longer work some time after the first article appeared. The book was widely reviewed after it appeared, including such scholarly journals as *The American Journal of Sociology*, *The Annals of the American Academy*, and *The Journal of Political Economy*, as well as the more political *New Republic*, the social policy-oriented *Survey*, and the *Sunday Book Review* section of the widely read *New York Times*. Her book appeared in the fall of 1915, at a time when America was slowly moving closer to war and the Progressive era was at its apex.

From the first, *The House on Henry Street* was considered a significant work. The reviewer in the *New Republic* noted, however, that the "book has no particular mood. It is inexpert in its anecdotes of the neighborhood, somewhat temporalizing in many of its judgments. But it is. . . a magnificent record of volition."[4] The reviewer in the *Survey* found the style more pleasing. "Miss Wald's book grasps the attention of the reader less by artificial word painting than by lucidity and directness. So simple is the style, so intimate is the appeal that the reader feels that the book was especially written for him."[5] It remained however, for the more scholarly *Annals of the American Academy* to make the almost inevitable comparison to the work of Jane Addams, stating, "In as significant a contribution to the literature of the settlement movement as Miss Addams' similar work. *Twenty Years at Hull House*, another leading woman of America has told the absorbing annals of *The House on Henry Street*."[6]

If *The House on Henry Street* was written in a simple style, it nonetheless tells a complex story. As most reviewers recognized at the time, it is both a story of one woman's indomitable nature, and the story of a special institution in a particular neighborhood of New York City; as well as a reflection of the spirit of an optimistic era in which the actors participated in larger social and political changes in our country. It was not a chronology, rather, as one of the reviewers stated, a history[7] - one that moved easily from the personal, through the community, and finally to the national levels of American government.

Henry Street Settlement was founded in 1893, one of the early group of American settlements that started after the development of Toynbee Hall, the first settlement, in England. However, Lillian Wald, by her own admission, had no knowledge of the other settlements when she began her work, and she plunged into action because she felt driven to do so. The following event opens the book: the author, a nurse, had been teaching classes to women about home nursing. During one of the classes, a young child called her to the bedside of a sick woman. Miss Wald's outrage at the "wretched" condition of the girl's sick mother led her to quit her advanced nursing studies on the spot. Soon after, she had enlisted the aid of a fellow nurse, Marie M. Brewster, in opening up a resident nursing service in the impoverished lower East Side neighborhood. Characteristically, Lillian Wald acted quickly. There was little time given to long-range reflection before the two women moved into their simple, furnished apartment. As Jacob Riis described the incident twenty years later, after Lillian Wald saw that sick woman, "she did not shut the door and go right away to report the case to the Board of Health. She went right to work to do what she could for the sick woman with what she had. . . ."[8] Unlike Jane Addams, Lillian Wald tended not to be introspective, but like Jane Addams she mobilized herself and others quickly to redress perceived wrong and injustice.[9]

Marie Brewster moved into Henry Street with Lillian Wald but left a few years later to get married; she died shortly afterward. By that time, the Settlement, which had been called the Nurses' Settlement, had already begun to broaden its range of activities from the local neighborhood to the city and even to the nation's capital.[10]

This was an early example of the social work practice of going from case to cause. When problems in the neighborhood could not be adequately resolved there, help might still be offered to an individual or a family on a case basis. But for more permanent solutions for groups of oppressed people, settlement leaders went to City Hall, to Congress, even to the President of the United States. Political action often involved them in controversy, but settlement workers understood the connection between the conditions of misery surrounding them and the need for larger-scale social reform. They made a conscious connection between residence in the community and the data provided by their social experiments. This served as an important means of proving that legislative and political reform was necessary.

Although Lillian Wald was unaware of the settlement movement when she moved into an apartment on the lower East Side, she was nonetheless following a path that paralleled that of other young men and women concerned about the plight of poor immigrants in our country. By the time she had moved into 265 Henry Street, in the building that was to be a home for her and many others, Lillian Wald had embarked on a path which overlapped with that of other educated people, primarily women, who took up community work and social reform as a lifetime occupation. What would today be called a network of influential people soon developed. Colleagues such as Florence Kelly and Paul Kellogg (editor of the *Survey*) moved from city to city, and particularly between Hull House in Chicago and Henry Street in New York. Jane Addams and Lillian Wald developed a relationship that continued throughout their lives, sustained by correspondence and through mutual interests and common activities, including participation in meetings around the woman's labor movement and the struggle for peace.

There was an objective necessity for the activities of the Settlement when poverty, poor working conditions, and inequality existed despite general prosperity and an expanding economy. But there was also what Jane Addams described as a "subjective necessity" in the founding of the settlements and in the life of community service which women like Ms. Wald undertook.[11] The settlements plainly served as a place for college-educated women who were not content to play out traditional roles of daughter and mother by the hearth at home. Rather, these women wanted to use their training and knowledge for an enlightened purpose, in the spirit of the Progressive era. The settlements allowed such women, like Miss Wald, to replicate backgrounds they could not completely abandon. They adopted a communal style of living similar to the dormitories of their happy college years, and they incorporated the comfortable environment of the bourgeois home in their urban residences, while engaging in socially useful activities.

Lillian Wald became a popular, well-known figure in the Henry Street Settlement neighborhood. The Settlement itself was described as surrounded by small children and young people whom she attracted to its programs.[12] With Lillian Wald as head worker, the programs proliferated, from the first nursing visits to the sick and poor, to clubs for young people with a variety of activities and focus, to the development of Clinton Hall as a separate meeting and party place for the young people in the neighborhood (drink-and politics-free, unlike the meeting places provided by the beer parlor and Tammany Hall). The book tells the story of the growth of these activities. In fact, the number of chapters devoted to children and youth (seven, or nearly half the book) reveals the significance placed on helping young people grow, develop and thrive in this inhospitable urban environment. In this context, the settlement gave scholarships to young people to help them pursue their studies. As a case in point, the drawings in the book were produced by one of the young artists who received assistance in developing his talents as a printmaker through a fellowship offered by Henry Street Settlement.[13]

The settlement movement is closely associated with the emergence of the social work profession, and although she was trained as a nurse, Lillian Wald has been described as a social worker by bibliographers, historians, and early reviewers of her book. Mainly, however, historians have concluded that the work of the settlement movement progressed as it did, and enjoyed the freedom to explore a wide variety of actions, and take on City Hall, because it was primarily non-professional. Most of the work in its early formative years was carried out by volunteers, or people, like Lillian Wald, who were not entirely dependent upon settlement revenues for their livelihood. In fact, the idea of institutionalization of the settlements was an anathema to many of the early settlement leaders, and certainly to Miss Wald. She resisted incorporation of the Settlement until 1903, and she prevented the house on 265 from becoming too big by locating programs in separate buildings as these activities proliferated. The settlements were supposed to make an impact on the institutions around them, not to become institutions themselves. Nevertheless, Henry Street Settlement achieved a certain status, and Lillian Wald attracted prestigious backers, including members of the powerful Jewish philanthropic and banking families of the Warburgs, Schiffs, and Loebs, who supported the Settlement through Board activity and donations. A later description in the *International Encyclopedia of Social Services* noted that "Wald's ability to express her enthusiasm for the Settlement's programs made her a talented fundraiser." As one friend observed, "It costs five thousand dollars to sit next to her at dinner."[14] In a sense, this underscores the point made by several reviewers. It was apparently accurate, if ironic, that as F.H. expressed it in *The New Republic*, "It is as an executive that Miss Wald impresses me."[15]

Lillian Wald was born in Cincinnati, Ohio on March 19, 1867, but she spent most of her early years in Rochester, New York. She was the second daughter and third of four children of Max D. Wald, a dealer in optical goods, and Minnie (Schwarz) Wald. Her father had immigrated from Germany. Her mother, whose origins were Polish, was a strong-minded woman with charitable interests, who also lived at Henry Street for some years before her death in 1923. Their family was close-knit, and included a grandfather and an uncle who were strong influences on Miss Wald's childhood. The Wald family was Jewish, but apparently religion did not play a major role in their lives.

Lillian Wald attended Miss Cruttenden's "English and French Boarding and Day School for Young Ladies and Little Girls." After graduation she applied for admission to Vassar College but was rejected on grounds that she was too young. She spent the next six years engaged in social activities, travel and some abortive career attempts. Thereafter, inspired by the efforts of a nurse who cared for a sick sister, Lillian Wald decided to undertake the nursing career that eventually led her to residence on Henry Street.

The story of Lillian Wald's work at Henry Street is told in *The House on Henry Street*, but her personal accomplishments went far beyond that neighborhood. In 1912 she received the gold medal of the National Institute of Social Sciences and later the Rotary Club's medal "in recognition of lifelong service, as sociologist, organizer and publicist."[16] She was instrumental in the child welfare movement, was part of the pacifist group that included Florence Kelley and Jane Addams of Hull House, and was conversant with several American presidents. Lillian Wald was, as always, helpful when needed, and in 1918 during a flu epidemic in New York City she chaired the Nurses' Emergency Council. After World War I, she founded the League of Free Nations Association (now known as the Foreign Policy Association), and visited the Soviet Union in 1924. Despite her active life, Lillian Wald found the time to produce significant reports on social issues, such as "Boarded-Out Babies" (1907) and "Sanitary Control of an Industry by the Industry Itself" (1913) - issues that remain of concern today. And in addition to *The House on Henry Street*, she also wrote *Windows on Henry Street* (1934), while recuperating from a major illness. She spent the last years of her life in Westport, Connecticut.

Perhaps for ideological reasons, the reviewer of *The House on Henry Street* in *The New Republic* emphasized more the community services role of the Settlement than its broader impact in effecting social change. This was true despite evidence that by 1916, when the review was printed, privately sponsored activities that started on the lower East Side had changed practices and policies of major public organizations in the nation as well as locally. As F.H. noted, "The experience of the social worker is often utilized by the state."[17] The reviewers in the *New York Times* and in *Survey* were more explicit about Miss Wald's role. The latter suggested that the book shows how *The House on Henry Street* "became a sort of moral powerhouse which sent reform currents in every direction." This would include the specific influence of Henry Street Settlement in the establishment of a nursing service in the public schools, the extensive use of the schools as social centers for the neighborhood, and the pervasiveness of Miss Wald's continuing battle to have the schools used as polling places for election (only adopted later).

On a broader scale, Henry Street Settlement played a significant part in improving working conditions of men, women and children. It was represented on the Joint Board of Sanitary Control (established by the manufacturers and workers in the cloak and suit industry), and the Settlement leadership influenced the founding of the New York State Bureau of Industry and Immigration by Governor Charles Evans Hughes.

The litany of Henry Street initiatives leading to new institutions or to improvements of old ones is a long one. Many of these changes had a permanent impact on social and economic conditions in the city, state and nation. This began with that first non-sectarian nursing service, which led to the founding of a permanent voluntary organization, eventually known as the Visiting Nurse Service of New York City. The Settlement developed a playground, and that inspired other playgrounds for children in the city. It pioneered the establishment of ungraded classes for the mentally retarded. It also started the Neighborhood Playhouse, where according to the reviewer in the *New York Times*, "neighborhood players present poetic spectacles and modern plays." Unlike other settlements, black people were welcome at Henry Street, although the settlement in addition had a special branch which served "Negroes" elsewhere.

If the settlement residents and Lillian Wald were involved with recreation and the arts, they were also interested in political action and Big Ideas. The heart of the settlement movement was its flexibility and ability to encompass diverse activities and concerns, from the "minutiae" of everyday life and Americanization of immigrants by moral example, to the larger questions of social justice. Henry Street Settlement was host to meetings that led to the formation of women's trade unions, and to meetings of the American branch of the Friends of Russian Freedom. Katharine Brehskovsky, "Babuschka" (little grandmother), the Russian anarchist, visited Henry Street and received encouragement from her friendship with Lillian Wald. Settlement leaders and their friends provided social services but they did not shirk overt political activity. They helped elect candidates and met with Presidents, including Theodore Roosevelt, Woodrow Wilson, and later Franklin Roosevelt. When Lillian Wald and Florence Kelley met with Theodore Roosevelt, they initiated the formation of the Federal Children's Bureau, (actually established under President Taft), and which Miss Wald described as a "symbol of the most helpful aspect of America."[18]

Lillian Wald took some controversial positions that at times alienated her rich and influential supporters. Of particular controversy was her aid to the Progressive Party, involvement with a garment maker's strike, and commitment to pacifism prior to the United States entry into World War I. Once decided on the issue of the peace movement, Miss Wald took a leadership role, and in 1915 she became the first president of the American Union Against Militarism. Subsequently, she spoke against preparedness before the Senate Military Committee, and was part of the seven-person delegation from the Union Against Militarism that met with President Wilson.

However, she was also adaptable. After the United States entered the war, Lillian Wald became a subcommittee member of the Council of National Defense. In later years Eleanor Roosevelt visited with her, and Lillian Wald was invited to co-chair, along with the philanthropist George Foster Peabody, a committee of the Good Neighbor League, whose purpose was to bring "non-political people into the campaign" of Roosevelt in 1936.[19] By that time she was in semi-retirement, but her credibility clearly remained untarnished.

Lillian Wald and *The House on Henry Street* frequently seemed to be undistinguishable, even after the activities of the Settlement led to bigger reforms. Indeed, the work of The Henry Street Settlement in the years covered in the book, 1893-1915, and until her resignation from Henry Street's leadership in 1933, directly reflects the *impramateur* of Lillian Wald. The neighborhood base certainly provided the roots for understanding of the problems of immigrants. Most of the reforms emanating from the Settlement also had a larger, more permanent impact on conditions of women and children, through such institutions as public health nursing, labor and the New York City school systems. They were carried out as part of the reform impulses of the Progressive era, and were often done in coordination with others, including trade unionists or even more conservative professionals such as Edward Devine, head of the New York School of Philanthropy.

But that is not to underplay the special role of Lillian Wald, whose personality and character played a key part in effecting these changes. Lillian Wald was enthusiastic, more compromising, and apparently more flexible than Florence Kelley. She was clearly an asset in controversial situations or meetings with national leaders and presidents. Her ability to energize others, and to mingle with elite lay people as well as revolutionaries, enabled her to make a lasting contribution to the causes she adopted, and to the institution of Henry Street itself. Like Jane Addams, feminism was not her primary cause. However, she was an outspoken suffragist, and some of her words seem more akin to feminism than has generally been recognized. For example, she said in a speech at Vassar College, "upon the educated woman, . . . devolves the task of readapting the social interests of her gender to a changed physical and spiritual environment. Colleges and professional schools have prepared the way for the citizenship of women, as have also the factories and the department stores. . . ."[20]

Lillian Wald's personal qualities gained her the respect and affection of a variety of people. In a *New York Times* article, March 13, 1937, Paul Kellogg compared her with Edison, Ford and Burbank. "My belief is . . . that in improving, modifying, blending, creating, Miss Wald has shown gifts kindred to this triumvirate, and the conditions she has had to work under have been more taxing." Another of her close friends in the residence expressed her deep affection for Miss Wald, saying, "As I look back, I marvel at the sunniness. If there was ever a tinge of melancholy or sadness, it never showed."[21] Certainly, as at least one reviewer pointed out when the book first appeared, the author wrote with humor, and she attacked the world with courage.

How much Lillian Wald was admired and beloved by residents of the Settlement and the community surrounding it was made clear by Helen Hall, who succeeded her as Director of the Settlement in 1933. Hall showed sensitivity to the circumstances of taking over from Lillian Wald, reporting the feeling of a young man from one of the clubs who said club members had not expected to like the new director. Helen Hall described the difficulties she faced because "they had loved Miss Wald so much that they felt they just couldn't like me. Happily. . . they were having to give up the luxury of disliking me." If the boys were converted readily, it was not always that easy, however, and she was told that "one resident cried herself to sleep at the thought of having my furniture moved into what had been Miss Wald's apartment."[22]

Although ill in the 1930s, Lillian Wald continued to work as she was able, only gradually giving up the reins of Henry Street, going from head worker to president, and finally turning the presidency of the Board over to Jacob Schiff in October 1937. Meanwhile, by 1934, she completed her book, *Windows on Henry Street*, which concluded the story of Henry Street to that date, reflecting changes in the community and adding details of the Depression and her further involvement with politicians and public officials. In 1937, a playground near Henry Street was dedicated to her, with Mayor Fiorello LaGuardia, Helen Hall, and Mrs. Felix Warburg officiating at the ceremonies. The commemorative plaque stated:

> This playground
> is named for
> Lillian D. Wald
> in appreciation
> of her pioneer work
> for children
> and district nursing
> in this city.[23]

In 1943, Henry Street Settlement celebrated its 50th anniversary, but Lillian Wald did not live to be there. She died on September 1, 1940. Her obituary in the *New York Times* extolled her many accomplishments, for the lower East Side and the nation, and cited explicitly her books as "classics in their field." In 1940 articles about Miss Wald's career appeared in *Social Service Review* and the *American Journal of Public*

Health. The best known biographies of Lillian Wald are those by R. L. Dufus, *Lillian Wald: Neighbor and Crusader* (Macmillan, 1938) and B. W. Epstein, *Lillian Wald: Angel of Henry Street* (J. Messner, 1948).

Henry Street Settlement has been, and is still, a part of the story of New York City, and as such its national influence seems at times to have been obscured. Nevertheless, its development is part of the growth of social work in our country, as well as integrally related to the story of progressivism and social reform nationwide. Thus, the archives of Henry Street are to be found in the Social Welfare History Archives of the University of Minnesota in Minneapolis. The personal papers of Lillian Wald are in New York, in the rare books and manuscript Division of the New York Public Library and at Columbia University. Assessment of the legacy of Lillian Wald finally has to be seen in relation to the settlement as well as through her personal history, and it should be noted that in 1990 Henry Street Settlement was still flourishing, with a $13 million operating budget.

Although it remains one of the leaders in the settlement field, Henry Street Settlement, like other settlements, has become primarily a service institution, rather than an instrument for major social reform and political activism. It is now serving primarily Black and Hispanic American who have replaced the earlier predominant groups of Jewish, Italian and Irish immigrants in the lower East Side. After a brief period of renewed activism, in connection with the Mobilization for Youth Program in the 1960s, Henry Street continues with a rich array of service activities, including recreation, cultural development, and employment programs, we well as housing programs. But settlements are no longer true leaders in shaping public policy. As a recent book expressed it, the settlement movement is currently caught in a sense of uncertainty.[24] Settlements are not significant forces for change in our society, and their involvement in the community is primarily through the work of professional staff. Henry Street is almost alone in having maintained a residence, in which the executive director lives with his family, and which houses occasional visitors.

In reading *The House on Henry Street* now, one is struck by the sense that the spirit of reform is no longer emanating from the settlements as it once did, nor indeed is the movement pervasive in our nation. Lillian Wald may perhaps have been premature when she said in the concluding pages of *The House on Henry Street* that "the settlements have been before the public long enough to have lost the glamour of moral adventure that was associated with the early days."[25] This may be more so as this book is being reissued. Much of the program for which Lillian Wald and her colleagues fought was accomplished; but "The Permanent War" against poverty and social injustice remains, and it is to be hoped that this book will remind us, and inspire us, to understand that the battle must continue.

Notes

1. In this essay, I refer to Lillian Wald as Miss Wald, in keeping with the practice utilized by the reviewers of the book when it was published, and which was the way she was generally called during her lifetime.

2. Personal interview with Daniel Kronenfeld, sixth Executive Director of Henry Street Settlement, April 1989.

3. Francis Tyson, review of *The House on Henry Street* in the *Annals of the American Academy of Political and Social Science* 64 (January 1916): 243.

4. F.H. (Francis Hackett), "The Permament War," review of *The House on Henry Street* in the *New Republic* 5 (8 January 1916): 255-56.

5. J. Salwyn Schapiro, "House on Henry Street," by Lillian Wald, review in *Survey*, 35, January 8, 1916: 437-438.

6. Tyson, review on *The House on Henry Street*, in the *Annals*, 243.

7. "Story of the House on Henry Street" review of *The House on Henry Street* in the *New York Times* (Book Review), 21 November 1916: p. 451.

8. Jacob Riis quotation is found in R.L. Dufus, *Lillian Wald: Neighbor and Crusader* (New York: Macmillan, 1938), 31.

9. This point about Lillian Wald is made in Dufus, *Lillian Wald*, p. 58 and throughout. The description of Jane Addams is to be found in Allen F. Davis, *American Heroine: The Life and Legend of Jane Addams* (New York: Oxford University Press, 1973), 158.

10. In an amusing story repeated in Dufus, Miss Wald said that the Settlement changed its name from "Nurses Settlement" to Henry Street Settlement because boys in the athletic club were being taunted by cries of "Noices!" Noices!" See Dufus, *Lillian Wald*, pp. 59-60.

11. Discussed in Jane Addams, *Twenty Years at Hull House* with autobiograhical notes and with illustrations by Norah Hamilton. (New York: Macmillan, 1910), 113-27.

12. Dufus, *Lillian Wald*, pp. 51-52. Also described in "Story of the House on Henry Street," review in the *New York Times*, 21 November, 1915, p. 451.

13. Several reviewers noted that the book contained etchings and drawings by Abraham Phillips, who was an artist from the community of the Settlement. See for example, the review by F. H. in the *New Republic*, who describes the book as "touchingly illustrated," and also the discussion in "An Etcher of Henry Street," in *Survey* 35, (6 November 1915): 136-40.

14. Quoted in William Wallach, "Henry Street Settlement," *Greenwood Encyclopedia of American Institutions* 1: *Social Service Organizations*, ed., Peter Romanofsky (Westport, Ct: Greenwood Press, 1978), 348.

15. R. H., "The Permanent War," review of *Henry Street* in *New Republic*, 8 January 1916, pp. 255-56.

16. From "Lillian Wald Dies: Friend of the Poor," Obituary in the *New York Times*, 3 September 1940: recent discussion about her career is to be found in the article by "S.B.W." on Lillian D. Wald in *American Reformers*, Alden Whitman, ed. (New York: H. W. Wilson, 1985). Other sources include the biographies cited in the text below.

17. F. H., "The Permanent War."

18. Wald, *The House on Henry Street*, with illustrations and photographs by Abraham Phillips and a new introduction by Helen Hall (Holt, Rinehart & Winston, 1915, reprint ed. New York: Dover Publications, 1971, 167.

19. Arthur M. Schlesinger, Jr., *The Age of Roosevelt*, vol. I: *The Politics of Upheaval* (Boston: Houghton Mifflin, 1960), 597.

20. "Asks Vassar Women to Uphold Ideals," *New York Times*, 13 October, 1915, p. 16.

21. Both quotations are given in Dufus, *Lillian Wald*, p. 346.

22. Helen Hall, *Unfinished Business in Neighborhood and Nation*, (New York: Macmillan, 1971), 7.

23. "Lillian Wald Dies: Friend of the Poor," Obituary of Lillian D. Wald, *New York Times*, 2 September 1940, p. 15.

24.   Judith Ann Trolander, *Professionals and Social Change: From the Settlement House Movement to Neighborhood Centers, 1886 to the Present* (New York: Columbia University Press, 1987).

25.   Wald, *The House on Henry Street*, (reprint ed. 1971), 309-10.

THE HOUSE ON HENRY STREET

THE HOUSE ON HENRY STREET

CHAPTER I

THE EAST SIDE TWO DECADES AGO

A SICK woman in a squalid rear tenement, so wretched and so pitiful that, in all the years since, I have not seen anything more appealing, determined me, within half an hour, to live on the East Side.

I had spent two years in a New York training-school for nurses; strenuous years for an undisciplined, untrained girl, but a wonderful human experience. After graduation, I supplemented the theoretical instruction, which was casual and inconsequential in the hospital classes twenty-five years ago, by a period of study at a medical college. It was while at the college that a great opportunity came to me.

I had little more than an inspiration to be of use in some way or somehow, and going to the hospital seemed the readiest means of realizing my desire. While there, the long hours " on duty " and the exhausting demands of the ward work scarcely admitted freedom for keeping informed as to what was happening in the world outside. The nurses had no time for general reading; visits to and from friends were brief; we were out of the current and saw little of life save as it flowed into the hospital wards. It is not strange, therefore, that I should have been ignorant of the various movements which reflected the awakening of the social conscience at the time, or of the birth of the "settlement," which twenty-five years ago was giving form to a social protest in England and America. Indeed, it was not until the plan of our work on the East Side was well developed that knowledge came to me of other groups of people who, reacting to a humane or an academic appeal, were adopting this mode of expression and calling it a "settlement."

Two decades ago the words "East Side" called up a vague and alarming picture of something strange and alien: a vast crowded area, a foreign city within our own, for whose conditions we had no concern. Aside from its exploiters, political and economic, few people had any definite knowledge of it, and its literary "discovery" had but just begun.

The lower East Side then reflected the popular indifference—it almost seemed contempt—for the living conditions of a huge population.

And the possibility of improvement seemed, when my inexperience was startled into thought, the more remote because of the dumb acceptance of these conditions by the East Side itself. Like the rest of the world I had known little of it, when friends of a philanthropic institution asked me to do something for that quarter.

Remembering the families who came to visit patients in the wards, I outlined a course of instruction in home nursing adapted to their needs, and gave it in an old building in Henry Street, then used as a technical school and now part of the settlement. Henry Street then as now was the center of a dense industrial population.

From the schoolroom where I had been giving a lesson in bed-making, a little girl led me one drizzling March morning. She had told me of her sick mother, and gathering from her incoherent account that a child had been born, I caught up the paraphernalia of the bed-making lesson and carried it with me. The child led me over broken roadways,—

there was no asphalt, although its use was well established in other parts of the city,—over dirty mattresses and heaps of refuse,—it was before Colonel Waring had shown the possibility of clean streets even in that quarter,—between tall, reeking houses whose laden fire-escapes, useless for their appointed purpose, bulged with household goods of every description. The rain added to the dismal appearance of the streets and to the discomfort of the crowds which thronged them, intensifying the odors which assailed me from every side. Through Hester and Division streets we went to the end of Ludlow; past odorous fish-stands, for the streets were a market-place, unregulated, unsupervised, unclean; past evil-smelling, uncovered garbage-cans; and—perhaps worst of all, where

so many little children played—past the trucks brought down from more fastidious quarters and stalled on these already overcrowded streets, lending themselves inevitably to many forms of indecency.

The child led me on through a tenement hallway, across a court where open and unscreened closets were promiscuously used by

men and women, up into a rear tenement, by
slimy steps whose accumulated dirt was aug-
mented that day by the mud of the streets,
and finally into the sickroom.

All the maladjustments of our social and
economic relations seemed epitomized in this
brief journey and what was found at the end
of it.   The family to which the child led me
was neither criminal nor vicious.   Although
the husband was a cripple, one of those who
stand on street corners exhibiting deformities
to enlist compassion, and masking the begging
of alms by a pretense at selling; although the
family of seven shared their two rooms with
boarders,—who were literally boarders, since
a piece of timber was placed over the floor for
them to sleep on,—and although the sick
woman lay on a wretched, unclean bed, soiled
with a hemorrhage two days old, they were
not degraded human beings, judged by any
measure of moral values.

In fact, it was very plain that they were
sensitive to their condition, and when, at the
end of my ministrations, they kissed my hands
(those who have undergone similar experiences
will, I am sure, understand), it would have
been some solace if by any conviction of the
moral unworthiness of the family I could have
defended myself as a part of a society which

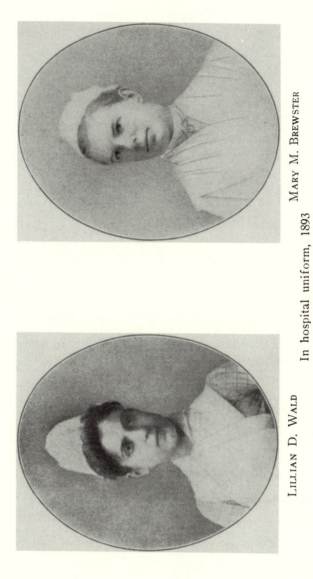

LILLIAN D. WALD   In hospital uniform, 1893   MARY M. BREWSTER

permitted such conditions to exist. Indeed,
my subsequent acquaintance with them revealed the fact that, miserable as their state
was, they were not without ideals for the family

life, and for society, of which they were so
unloved and unlovely a part.

That morning's experience was a baptism of
fire. Deserted were the laboratory and the
academic work of the college. I never returned to them. On my way from the sickroom to my comfortable student quarters my

mind was intent on my own responsibility. To my inexperience it seemed certain that conditions such as these were allowed because people did not *know*, and for me there was a challenge to know and to tell. When early morning found me still awake, my naive conviction remained that, if people knew things,—and "things" meant everything implied in the condition of this family,—such horrors would cease to exist, and I rejoiced that I had had a training in the care of the sick that in itself would give me an organic relationship to the neighborhood in which this awakening had come.

To the first sympathetic friend to whom I poured forth my story, I found myself presenting a plan which had been developing almost without conscious mental direction on my part. It was doubtless the accumulation of many reflections inspired by acquaintance with the patients in the hospital wards, and now, with the Ludlow Street experience, resistlessly impelling me to action.

Within a day or two a comrade from the training-school, Mary Brewster, agreed to share in the venture. We were to live in the neighborhood as nurses, identify ourselves with it socially, and, in brief, contribute to it our citizenship. That plan contained in embryo all the extended and diversified social interests of our settlement group to-day.

We set to work immediately to find quarters —no easy task, as we clung to the civilization of a bathroom, and ac-  cording to a legend current at the time there were only two bathrooms in tenement houses below Fourteenth Street. Chance helped us here. A young woman who for years played an important part in the life of many East Side people, overhearing a conversation of mine with a fellow-student, gave me an introduction to two men who, she said, knew all about the quarter of the city which I wished to enter. I called on them immediately, and their response to my need was as prompt. Without stopping to inquire into my antecedents or motives, or to discourse on the social aspects of the community, of which, I soon learned, they were competent to speak with authority, they set out with me at once, in a pouring rain, to scour the adjacent streets for " To Let " signs. One which seemed to me worth investigating my newly acquired friends discarded with the explanation that it was in the "red light" district and would not do.   Later I was to know much of the unfortunate women who inhabited the quarter, but at the time the term meant nothing to me.

After a long tour one of my guides, as if by inspiration, reminded the other that several young women had taken a house on Rivington Street for something like my purpose, and perhaps I had better live there temporarily and take my time in finding satisfactory quarters. Upon that advice I acted, and within a few days Miss Brewster and I found ourselves guests at the luncheon table of the College Settlement on Rivington Street.   With ready hospitality they took us in, and, during July and August, we were "residents" in stimulating comradeship with serious women, who were also the fortunate possessors of a saving sense of humor.

Before September of the year 1893 we found a house on Jefferson Street, the only one in which our careful search disclosed the desired bathtub.   It had other advantages—the vacant floor at the top (so high that the windows along the entire side wall gave us sun and breeze), and, greatest lure of all, the warm welcome which came to us from the basement, where we found the janitress ready to answer questions as to terms.

Naturally, objections to two young women living alone in New York under these conditions had to be met, and some assurance as to our material comfort was given to anxious, though at heart sympathetic, families by compromising on good furniture, a Baltimore heater for cheer, and simple but adequate household appurtenances. Painted floors with easily removed rugs, windows curtained with spotless but inexpensive scrim, a sitting-room with pictures, books, and restful chairs, a tiny bedroom which we two shared, a small dining-room in which the family mahogany did not look out of place, and a kitchen, constituted our home for two full years.

The much-esteemed bathroom, small and dark, was in the hall, and necessitated early rising if we were to have the use of it; for, as we became known, we had many callers anxious to see us before we started on our sick rounds. The diminutive closet-space was divided to hold the bags and equipment we needed from day to day, and more ample store-closets were given us by the kindly people in the school where I had first given lessons to East Side mothers. Any pride in the sacrifice of material comfort which might have risen within us was effectually inhibited by the constant reminder that we two young persons occupied exactly the same space as the large families on every floor below us, and to one of our basement friends at least we were luxurious beyond the dreams of ordinary folk.

The little lad from the basement was our first invited guest. The simple but appetizing dinner my comrade prepared, while I set the table and placed the flowers. The boy's mother came up later in the evening to find out what we had given him, for Tommie had rushed down with eyes bulging and had reported that "them ladies live like the Queen of England and eat off of solid gold plates."

We learned the most efficient use of the fire-escape and felt many times blessed because of our easy access to the roof. We also learned the infinite uses to which stairs can be put. Later we achieved "local color" in our rooms by the addition of interesting pieces of brass and copper purchased from a man on Allen Street whom we and several others had "dis-

covered." His little dark shop under the ele-
vated railway was fitfully illuminated by the
glowing forge. On our first visit the proprietor emerged from a still darker inner room
with prayer-shawl and phylactery. He became
one of our pleasant acquaintances and lost no
occasion of acknowledging what he considered

his debt to the appreciative customers who had
helped to make him and his wares known to a
wider circle than that of the neighborhood.

The mere fact of living in the tenement
brought undreamed-of opportunities for widen-
ing our knowledge and extending our human
relationships. That we were Americans was
wonderful to our fellow-tenants. They were
all immigrants—Jews from Russia or Rou-
mania. The sole exception was the janitress,
Mrs. McRae, who at once dedicated herself and
her entire family to the service of the top floor.
Dear Mrs. McRae! From her basement home

she covered us with her protecting love and was no small influence in holding us to sanity. Humor, astuteness, and sympathy were needed and these she gave in abundance.

It was vouchsafed us to know many fine personalities who influenced and guided us from the first few weeks of residence in the friendly college settlement through the many years that have followed. The two women who stand out with greatest distinction from the first are this pure-souled Scotch-Irish immigrant and Josephine Shaw Lowell. Both, if they were here, would understand the tribute in linking them together.

Occasionally Mrs. McRae would feel impelled to reprove us for " overdoing " ourselves, and from our top story we were hard pushed to save visitors from being sent away when she thought we needed to finish a meal or go to bed. Cautious as we were not to make any distinctions in commenting upon the visitors who came to see us, she made her own deductions. At whatever hour we returned, she would be at the door to welcome us and to report on the happenings during our absence. "So-and-so was here": shrewd descriptions which often enabled us to identify individuals when names were forgotten. "Lots of visitors to-night," she would report. "Were messages left, or names?" we would naturally inquire. "No, darlints, nothing at all. I know sure they didn't bring you anything."

The key to our apartments, usually left with her, was one day forgotten, and when, upon unlocking the door, we saw a well-known society woman seated in our little living-room, we were naturally puzzled to know how she had arrived there. Mrs. McRae explained that she had taken her up the fire-escape!—no slight venture and exertion for the inexperienced. We suggested that other ways might have been more agreeable and safer. "Whisht," said Mrs. McRae, with a smile and a wink, "it's no harm at all. She'll be havin' lots of talk for her friends on this."

When her roving husband died at home, the funeral arrangements were given a last touch by Mrs. McRae, who placed on the casket his tobacco and pipe and ordered the procession to pass his tenement home twice before driving to the cemetery, "So he'd not think we were not for forgivin' him and hurryin' him away."

Her first love went to my comrade, whose

beauty and humor and goodness captured her Celtic heart. During our second year in the tenement Miss Brewster was taken seriously ill, and one evening we had at last succeeded in forcing Mrs. McRae to go home and had locked the door. Unknown to us the dear friend remained on the floor outside all through the night, trying to catch the sound of life from the loved one.

Bringing up a large family, with no help from the " old man," and with stern ideals of conduct and integrity, was not easy. Some of her children, endowed with her character, gave her solace, but she was too astute not to estimate each one properly.

When we moved from the tenement to our first house Mrs. McRae and her family gave up the basement rooms, which were rent free because of her janitor service, in order to be near us, and she spread her warmth over the new abode. When, some years later, she was ill and we knew that the end was near, one close to me in my own family claimed my attention. Torn between the two affections, I was loath to leave the city while Mrs. McRae was so ill. She guessed the cause of my perturbed state and advised me to go. " Darlin', you ought to go. You go. I promise not to die until you come back."

Letters kept up this assurance and the promise was fulfilled.

Times were hard that year. In the summer the miseries due to unemployment and rising rents and prices began to be apparent, but the pinch came with the cold weather. Perhaps it was an advantage that we were so early exposed to the extraordinary sufferings and the variety of pain and poverty in that winter of 1893-94, memorable because of extreme economic depression. The impact of strain, physical and emotional, left neither place nor time for self-analysis and consequent self-consciousness, so prone to hinder and to dwarf wholesome instincts, and so likely to have proved an impediment to the simple relationship which we established with our neighbors.

It has become almost trite to speak of the kindness of the poor to each other, yet from the beginning of our tenement-house residence we were much touched by manifestations of it. An errand took me to Michael the Scotch-Irish cobbler as the family were sitting down to the noonday meal. There was a stranger with them, whom Michael introduced, explaining when we were out of hearing that he thought I would be interested to meet a man just out of Sing Sing prison. I expressed some fear of the danger to his own boys in this association. "We must just chance it," said Michael. "It's no weather for a man like that to be on the streets, when honest fellows can't get work."

When we first met the G—— family they were breaking up the furniture to keep from freezing. One of the children had died and had been buried in a public grave. Three times that year did Mrs. G—— painfully gather together enough money to have the baby disinterred and fittingly buried in consecrated ground, and each time she gave up her heart's desire in order to relieve the sufferings of the living children of her neighbors.

Another instance of this unfailing goodness of the poor to each other was told by Nellie, who called on us one morning. She was evidently embarrassed, and with difficulty related that, hearing of things to be given away at a newspaper office, she had gone there hoping to get something that would do for John when he came out of the hospital. She said, "I drew this and I don't know exactly what it is meant for," and displayed a wadded black satin "dress-shirt protector," in very good condition, and possibly contributed because the season was over! Standing outside the circle of clamorous petitioners, Nellie and the woman next her had exchanged tales of woe. When she mentioned her address the new acquaintance suggested that she seek us.

Nellie proved to be a near neighbor. There were two children: a nursing baby "none so well," and a lad. John, her husband, was "fortunately" in the hospital with a broken leg, for there were "no jobs around loose anyway." When we called later in the day to see the baby, we found that Nellie was stopping with her cousin, a widower who "held his job down." There were also his two children, the widow of a friend "who would have done as much by me," and the wife and two small children of a total stranger who lived in the rear tenement and were invited in to meals because the father had been seen starting every morning on his hunt for work, and "it was plain for anyone with eyes to see that he never did get it." So this one man, fortunate in having work, was taking care of himself and his children, the widow of his friend, Nellie and her children, and was feeding the strangers. Said Nellie: "Sure he's doing that, and why not? He's the only cousin I've got outside of Ireland."

Mrs. S——, who called at the settlement a few days ago, reminded me that it was twenty-one years since our first meeting, and brought vividly before me a picture of which she was a part. She was the daughter of a learned rabbi, and her husband, himself a pious man, had great reverence for the traditions of her family. In their extremity they had taken bread from one of the newspaper charities, but it was evi-

dently a painful humiliation, and before we arrived they had hidden the loaf in the ice-box. My visit was due to a desire to ascertain the condition of the families who had applied for this dole. Both house and people were scrupulously clean. It was amazing that under the biting pressure of want and anxiety such standards could be maintained. Yet, though passionately devoted to his family, the husband refused advantageous employment because it necessitated work on the Sabbath. This would have been to them a desecration of something more vital than life itself.

We found that winter, in other instances, that the fangs of the wolf were often decorously hidden. In one family of our acquaintance the father, a cigarmaker, left the house each morning in search of work, only to return at night hungrier and more exhausted by his fruitless exertions. One Sabbath eve I entered his tenement, to find the two rooms scrubbed and cleaned, and the mother and children prepared for the holy night. Over a brisk fire fed by bits of wood picked up by the children two covered pots were set, as if a supper were being prepared. But under the lids it was only water that bubbled. The proud mother could not bear to expose her poverty to the gossip of the neighbors, the humiliation being the greater because she was obliged to violate the sacred custom of preparing a ceremonious meal for the united family on Friday night.

If the formalism of our neighbors in religious matters was constantly brought to our attention, instances of their tolerance were also far from rare. A Jewish woman, exhausted by her long day's scrubbing of office floors, walked many extra blocks to beg us to get a priest for her Roman Catholic neighbor whose child was dying. An orthodox Jewish father, who had been goaded to bitterness because his daughter had married an " Irisher " and thus " insulted his religion," felt that the young husband and his mother were equally wronged. This man, when I called on a Sabbath evening, took one of the lights from the table to show the way down the five flights of dark tenement stairs, and to my protest,—knowing, as I did, that he considered it a sin to handle fire on the Sabbath,—he said: "It is no sin for me to handle a light on the Sabbath to show respect to a friend who has helped to keep a family together."

There was the story of Mary, eldest daughter, as we supposed, of an orthodox family. When we went to her engagement party we were surprised to see that the young man was not of the family faith. The mother told us that Mary, "such a pretty baby," had been left on their doorstep in earlier and more prosperous days in Austria. "The Burgomeister had made proclamation," but no one came to claim her, and the husband and wife, who as yet had no children of their own, decided to keep her. "God rewarded us and answered our prayers," said Mrs. L——, for many children came afterward; but Mary, blonde and blue-eyed, was always the most cherished, the first-comer who had brought the others. When she was quite a young girl she was taken ill—a cold following exposure after her first "grown-up" party, for which her foster-mother had dressed her with pride. It seemed that nothing could save her, and the foster-mother in her distress thought with pity of the woman who had borne

With Prayer-shawl and Phylactery

this sweet child.   Surely she must be dead.   No
living mother could have abandoned so lovely
a baby.   And if she were dead and in the Chris-
tian heaven, she would look in vain there for

her daughter.   "So I called the priest and told
him," said Mrs. L——, "and he made a prayer
over Mary, and said, ' Now she is a *Krist.*'   The
doctor, we called him too, and he said to get
a goat, for the milk would be good for Mary;
and she get well, but no so strong, as you see,
and that is why she don't go out to work like
her brothers and sisters.   We lose our money,
that's why we come to America, and Mary,
now she marry a *Krist.*"

Gradually there came to our knowledge difficulties and conflicts not peculiar to any one set of people, but intensified in the case of our neighbors by poverty, unfamiliarity with laws and customs, the lack of privacy, and the frequent dependence of the elders upon the children. Workers in philanthropy, clergymen, orthodox rabbis, the unemployed, anxious parents, girls in distress, troublesome boys, came as individuals to see us, but no formal organization of our work was effected till we moved into the house on Henry Street, in 1895.

So precious were the intimate relationships with our neighbors in the tenement that we were reluctant to leave it. My companion's breakdown, the persuasion of friends who had given their support and counsel that there was an obligation upon us to effect some kind of formal organization without further delay, finally prevailed. As usual the neighborhood showed its interest in what we did; and though my comrade and I had carefully selected men from the ranks of the unemployed to move our belongings, when all was accomplished not one of them could be induced to take a penny for the work.

From this first house have since developed the manifold activities in city and country now incorporated as the Henry Street Settlement.

I should like to make it clear that from the beginning we were most profoundly moved by the wretched industrial conditions which were constantly forced upon us. In succeeding chapters I hope to tell of the constructive programmes that the people themselves have evolved out of their own hard lives, of the ameliorative measures, ripened out of sympathetic comprehension, and, finally, of the social legislation that expresses the new compunction of the community.

CHAPTER II

ESTABLISHING THE NURSING SERVICE

When I first entered the training-school my outpourings to the superintendent,—a woman touched with a genius for sympathy,—my youthful heroics, and my vow to " nurse the poor " were met with what I deemed vague reference to the " Mission." Afterwards when I sought guidance I found that in New York the visiting (or district) nurse was accessible only through sectarian organizations or the free dispensary.

As our plan crystallized my friend and I were certain that a system for nursing the sick in their homes could not be firmly established unless certain fundamental social facts were recognized. We tried to imagine how loved ones for whom we might be solicitous would react were they in the place of the patients whom we hoped to serve. With time, experience, and the stimulus of creative minds our technique and administrative methods have naturally improved, but this test gave us vision to establish certain principles, whose soundness has been proved during the growth of the service.

We perceived that it was undesirable to condition the nurse's service upon the actual or potential connection of the patient with a religious institution or free dispensary, or to have the nurse assigned to the exclusive use of one physician, and we planned to create a service on terms most considerate of the dignity and independence of the patients. We felt that the nursing of the sick in their homes should be undertaken seriously and adequately; that instruction should be incidental and not the primary consideration; that the etiquette, so far  as doctor and patient were concerned, should be analogous to the established system of private nursing; that the nurse should be as ready to respond to calls from the people themselves as to calls from physicians; that she should accept calls from all physicians, and with no more red-tape or formality than if she were to remain with one patient continuously.

The new basis of the visiting-nurse service which we thus inaugurated reacted almost immediately upon the relationship of the nurse to the patient, reversing the position the nurse had formerly held. Chagrin at having the neighbors see in her an agent whose presence proclaimed the family's poverty or its failure to give adequate care to its sick member was changed to the gratifying consciousness that her presence, in conjunction with that of the doctor, " private " or " Lodge," [1] proclaimed the family's liberality and anxiety to do everything possible for the sufferer. For the exposure of poverty is a great humiliation to people who are trying to maintain a foothold in society for themselves and their families.

My colleague and I realized that there were large numbers of people who could not, or would not, avail themselves of the hospitals. It was estimated that ninety per cent. of the sick people in cities were sick at home,—an estimate which has been corroborated (1913-14) by the investigation of the Committee of Inquiry into the Departments of Health, Charities, and Bellevue and Allied Hospitals of New York,—and a humanitarian civilization demanded that something of the nursing care given in hospitals should be accorded to sick people in their homes.

We decided that fees should be charged when

[1] The "Lodge" doctor is the physician provided by a mutual benefit society or " Lodge " to attend its members.—THE AUTHOR.

THE NURSE IN THE TENEMENT
Ninety per cent. of the sick of the city remain at home

people could pay. It was interesting to discover that, although nominal in amount compared with the cost of the service, these fees represented a much larger proportion of the wage in the case of the ordinary worker who paid for the hourly service than did the fee paid by a man with a salary of $5,000, who engaged the full time of the nurse. Our plan, we reasoned, was analogous to the custom of "private" hospitals, which give free treatment or charge according to the resources of the ward patients. Both private hospitals and visiting nursing are thereby lifted out of "charity" as comprehended by the people.

We felt that for economic reasons valuable and expensive hospital space should be saved for those for whom the hospital treatment is necessary; and an obvious social consideration was that many people, particularly women, cannot leave their homes without imperiling, or sometimes destroying, the home itself.

Almost immediately we found patients who needed care, and doctors ready to accept our services with probably the least amount of friction possible under the circumstances; for those doctors who had not been internes in the hospitals were unfamiliar with the trained nurse, whose work was little known at that time outside the hospitals and the homes of the well-to-do.

Despite the neighborhood's friendliness, however, we struggled, not only with poverty and disease, but with the traditional fate of the pioneer: in many cases we encountered the inevitable opposition which the unusual must arouse. It seems almost ungracious to relate some of our first experiences with doctors. No one can give greater tribute than do the nurses of the settlement to the generosity of physicians and surgeons when we recall how often paying patients were set aside for more urgent non-paying ones; the counsel freely given from the highest for the lowliest; the eager readiness to respond. Occasionally sage advice came from a veteran who knew the people well and lamented the economic pressure which at times involved, to their spiritual disaster, doctors as well as patients.

The first day on which we set out to discover the sick who might need a nurse, my comrade found a woman with high temperature in an airless room, more oppressive because of the fetid odor from the bed. Service with one of

New York's skilled specialists had trained the nurse well and she identified the symptoms immediately. " Yes, there was a Lodge doctor.— He had left a prescription.—He might come again." With fine diplomacy an excuse was

made to call upon the doctor and to assume that he would accept the nurse's aid. My colleague presented her credentials and offered to accompany him to the case immediately, as she was " sure conditions must have changed since his last visit or he would doubtless have ordered " so-and-so,—suggesting the treatment the distinguished specialists were then using. He promised to go, and the nurse waited patiently for hours at the woman's bedside. When he arrived he pooh-poohed and said, " Nothing doing." We had ascertained the financial condition of the family from the evidence of the empty push-cart and the fact that the fish-peddler was not in the market with his merchandise. Five dollars was loaned that night to purchase stock next day.

My comrade and I decided to visit the patient early the next morning, to mingle judgments on what action could be taken in this serious illness with due respect to established etiquette. When we arrived, the Lodge doctor and a " Professor " (a consultant) were in the sickroom, and our five dollars, left for fish, was in their possession. Cigarettes in mouths and hats on heads, they were questioning husband and wife, and only Dickens could have done justice to the scene. We were not too timid to allude to the poverty and the source of the fee, and felt free when we were told to " go ahead and do anything you like." That permission we acted upon instantly and received, over the telephone, authority from the distinguished specialist to get to work. We were prudent enough to report the authority and treatment given, with solemn etiquette, to the physician in attendance, who in turn congratulated us on having helped him to save a life!

Not all our encounters with this class of practitioner were fruitful of benefit to their patients. Heartbreaking was the tragedy of Samuel, the twenty-one-year-old carpenter, and Ida, his bride. They had been boy and girl sweethearts in Poland, and the coming to America, the preparation of the clean two-roomed home, the expectation of the baby, made a pretty story which should have had happy succeeding chapters, the start was so good. Samuel knocked at our door, incoherent in his fright, but we were fast accustoming ourselves to recognize danger-signals, and I at once followed him to the top floor of his tenement.

Plain to see, Ida was dying. The midwife said she had done all she could, but she was obviously frightened. " No one could have done any better," she insisted, " not any doctor "; but she had called one and he had left the woman lacerated and agonizing because the expected fee had been paid only in part. It was Samuel's last dollar. The septic woman could only be sent to the city hospital. The ambulance surgeon was persuaded to let the boy husband ride with her, and he remained at the hospital until she and the baby died a few hours later.

Here my comrade and I came against the

stone wall of professional etiquette. It seemed as if public sentiment ought to be directed by the doctors themselves against such practices, but although I finally called upon one of the high-minded and distinguished men who had signed the diploma of the offending doctor, I could not get reproof administered, and my ardor for arousing public indignation in the profession was chilled. Later, when I heard protests from employers against insistence by labor organizations on the closed shop, it occurred to me that they failed to recognize analogies in the professional etiquette which conventional society has long accepted.

However, many friendly strong bonds were made and have been sustained with a large majority of the doctors during all the years of our service. We have mutual ties of personal and community interests, and work together as comrades; the practitioners with high standards for themselves and ideals for their sacred profession comprehend our common cause and strengthen our hands. It is rare now, although at first it was very frequent, that the physician who has called in the nurse for his patient demands her withdrawal when he himself has been dismissed. He has come to see that although the nurse exerts her influence to preserve his prestige, for the patient's sake as well as his own, nevertheless, emotional people, unaccustomed to the settled relation of the family doctor, may and often do change physicians from six to ten times in the course of one illness. The nurse, however, may remain at the bedside throughout all vicissitudes.

The most definite protest against the newer relationship came from a woman active in many public movements, who was a stickler for the orthodox method of procuring a visiting nurse only through the doctor. To illustrate the importance of freedom for the patients, I cited the case of the L—— family. A neighbor had called for aid. " Some kind of an awful catching sickness on the same floor I live on, to the right, front," she whispered. A worn and haggard woman was lifting a heavy boiler filled with " wash " from the stove when I entered; on the floor in the other room three little children lay ill with typhoid fever, one of them with meningitis. The feather pillows, most precious possession, had been pawned to pay the doctor. The father dared not leave the shop, for money was needed, and all that he earned was far from enough. The mother, when questioned as to the delay in sending for nursing help, said that the doctor had frightened her from doing so by telling her that, if a nurse came, the children would surely be sent to the hospital. No disinfectant was found in the house, and the mother declared that no instructions had been given her.

The nurse who took possession of the sick-room refrained from mentioning the hospital; but when the mother saw the skilled ministration, and the tired father, on his return from work, watched the deft feeding of the unconscious child, they awoke to their limitations. The poor, unskilled woman, bent with fatigue, then exclaimed, " O God, is that what I should have been doing for my babies?" When the nurse was about to leave them for the night the parents clung to her and asked her if a hospital would do as much as she had done. "More, much more, I hope," she said. "I cannot give here what the little ones need." Late at night three carriages started for the children's ward of the hospital; the father, the mother, the nurse, each with a patient across the seat of the carriage.

Said the critic when I had finished my story: " I think the nurse should have asked permission of their doctor before she granted the request of the parents."

All the social agencies combined have not been able to dislodge permanently the quack who preys upon ignorance and superstition. One day a teacher in a nearby school asked us to visit a pupil who was highly excited and un-controllable. The mother, when questioned, confessed that she had employed the " witch doctor " to exorcise the devil, who, he said, had taken possession of the girl. In our efforts to free the girl from this man's control I invoked the aid of the parish priest, suggesting that his powers were being usurped. The County Medical Society finally secured conviction of the " doctor " on the charge of practicing without a license.

In the Italian quarter this species still preys upon the superstitious fears of some of the people, and the secrecy involved in his " treatment " makes permanent riddance extremely difficult. The people on the whole, however, give remarkable response to the " American " custom of employing a regular practitioner and the visiting nurse.

In this country, unfortunately, we have little data on morbidity. Statisticians desirous of obtaining figures for study have found interesting material in our files, and it has been possible to make comparison of the results of hospital and home treatment. Those who are familiar with the discussion upon papers presented by children's specialists in recent conferences on the saving of child life have had their attention drawn to the disadvantage of institutional treatment. Discussion of this subject is recent, and the laity do not always know that certain complications incident to the hospital care of children are obviated by keeping them at home. Among these are cross-infections, while the high mortality among infants in hospitals has long been recognized and deplored as unavoidable.

We soon found that children's diseases, particularly those of brief duration, lent themselves most advantageously to home treatment. Our records show that in 1914 the Henry Street staff cared for 3,535 cases of pneumonia of all ages, with a mortality rate of 8.05 per cent. For purposes of comparison four large New York hospitals gave us their records of pneumonia during the same period. Their combined figures totaled 1,612, with a mortality rate of 31.2 per cent. Among children under two—the age most susceptible to unfortunate termination of this disorder—the mortality rate from pneumonia in one hospital was 51 per cent., and the average of the four was 38 per cent., while among those of a corresponding age cared for by our nurses it was 9.3 per cent.

Doctors and nurses highly trained in hospital routine are apt to be hospital propagan-

dists until they learn by experience that there
is justification for the resistance, on the part of
mothers, to the removal of their children to in-

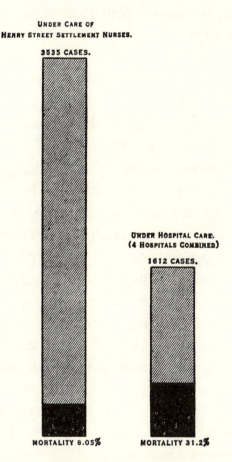

UNDER CARE OF
HENRY STREET SETTLEMENT NURSES.

3535 CASES.

UNDER HOSPITAL CARE.
(4 HOSPITALS COMBINED)

1612 CASES.

MORTALITY 8.05%   MORTALITY 31.2%

stitutions, and that even in homes which, at
first glance, it seems impossible to organize in
accordance with sickroom standards, the little
patients' chances for recovery are better than
when sent away. Diseases requiring climatic

or operative treatment, or peculiar apparatus, must usually be excluded from home care.

In a letter written to a friend more than twenty years ago I find this account of one of our patients:

" Peter had pneumonia, complicated with whooping-cough. He is a beautiful yellow-haired boy, and even if the hospital could have admitted him, or his mother would have agreed to his removal (which she wouldn't), I should not have liked to send him. The sense of re-sponsibility for the sick child seemed a force that could not be spared for rousing an erring father. He is, apparently, devoted to the child, but had been drinking, and there was not a dollar in the house. The child, desperately ill, clung to him, calling upon him with endearing names. During the illness he worked all day (he is a driver) and sat up all night, and I think he will never forget his shame and re-morse. The doctor had ordered bath treat-ments every two hours. These I gave until eight o'clock and the mother continued them after my last visit, but when the temperature was highest she was worn out, and active night-nursing seemed imperative. This Miss S—— willingly undertook—a service more difficult than appears in the mere telling, for the ver-

min in these old houses are horribly active at
night, and this sweet girl ended her first vigil
with neck and face inflamed from bites. Yet

Convalescent Home—"The Rest."

the people themselves were clean, and in this
were not blameworthy. There is nothing
harder to endure than to watch by a night sick-
bed in these old, worn houses and see the
crawling creatures and the babes so accustomed
to them that their sleep is scarcely disturbed.
Peter has had a beautiful recovery, rewarding
his nurses by a most satisfactory return to a
normal state of good health."

The staff, which in the beginning consisted
of two nurses, my friend and myself, has been
increased until it is now large enough to answer

calls from the sick anywhere in the boroughs of Manhattan and the Bronx, and the calls in the year 1913-14 came from nearly 1,100 more patients than the combined total of those treated during the same period in three of the large hospitals in New York—a comparison valuable chiefly as measuring the growing demand of the sick for the visiting nurse.

The service, though covering so wide a territory, is capable of control and supervision. The division into districts, with separate staffs for contagious and obstetrical cases, may be compared to the hospital division into wards. Like the hospital, it has a system of bedside notes, case records, and an established etiquette between physicians, nurses, and patients. Those that can best be cared for in the hospitals are sent there, the sifting process being accomplished by the doctors and nurses working together. Approximately ten per cent. of our patients are sent to the hospitals.

Serious nurses are gratified that the former casual and almost sentimental attitude of the public toward them and their work has been replaced by a demand for standards of efficiency.

Enthusiasm, health, and uncommon good sense on the part of the nurse are essential, for without the vision of the importance of their task they could not long endure the endless stair-climbing, the weight of the bag, and the pulls upon their emotions.

There has been an extraordinary development of the visiting-nurse service throughout the country since we began our rounds, and the practical arguments for sustaining such work would seem irresistible. It requires imagination, however, to visualize the steady, competent, continuous routine so quietly performed, unseen by the public, and its financial support is the more precarious because there can be no public reminder of its existence by impressive buildings and monuments of marble.

CHAPTER III

THE NURSE AND THE COMMUNITY

The work begun from the top floor of the tenement comprised, in simple forms, those varied lines of activity which have since been developed into the many highly specialized branches of public health nursing now covering the United States and engaging thousands of nurses.[1]

In trying to forestall every obstacle to the establishment of our nursing service on the East Side, it seemed desirable to have some connection with civic authority. Through a mutual friend I met the President of the Board of Health and, I fear rather presumptuously, asked that we be given some insignia. Desirous of serving his friend and tolerant of my intense earnestness, he sanctioned our wearing a badge which had engraved on its circle, " Visiting Nurse. Under the Auspices of the Board of Health."

As it transpired, we did not find it necessary

[1] "Visiting Nursing in the United States," by Y. G. Waters (Charities Publication Committee).

44

or always felicitous to utilize this privilege, but our connection with the Board of Health was not a perfunctory or merely complimentary one. We found from the beginning an inclination on the part of the officials of the department to treat us more or less like comrades. Every night, during the first summer, I wrote to the physician in charge, reporting the sick babies and describing the unsanitary conditions Miss Brewster and I found, and we received many encouraging reminders that what we were doing was considered helpful.

In the new activity for the promotion of public health many campaigns have been waged to popularize the study of social diseases. Education is the watchword, and where emphasis is laid upon the preservation of health rather than upon the treatment of disease, the nurses constitute an important factor. Appreciation of this is recorded by the Commission which drafted the new health law for New York State (1913). "The advent of trained nursing," says its report, "marks not only a new era in the treatment of the sick, but a new era in public health administration." This Commission also created the position of Director of the Division of Public Health Nursing in the state department of health.

I had been downtown only a short time when I met Louis. An open door in a rear tenement revealed a woman standing over a washtub, a fretting baby on her left arm, while with her right she rubbed at the butcher's aprons which she washed for a living.

Louis, she explained, was "bad." He did not "cure his head," and what would become of him, for they would not take him into the school because of it? Louis, hanging the offending head, said he had been to the dispensary a good many times. He knew it was awful for a twelve-year-old boy not to know how to read the names of the streets on the lamp-posts, but "every time I go to school Teacher tells me to go home."

It needed only intelligent application of the dispensary ointments to cure the affected area, and in September I had the joy of securing the boy's admittance to school for the first time in his life. The next day, at the noon recess, he fairly rushed up our five flights of stairs in the

Jefferson Street tenement to spell the elementary words he had acquired that morning.

It had been hard on Louis to be denied the precious years of school, yet one could sympathize with the harassed school teachers. The classes were overcrowded; there were frequently as many as sixty pupils in a single room, and often three children on a seat. It was, perhaps, not unnatural that the eczema on Louis's head should have been seized upon as a legitimate excuse for not adding him to the number. Perhaps it was not to be expected that the teacher should feel concern for one small boy whom she might never see again, or should realize that his brief time for education was slipping away and that he must go to work fatally handicapped because of his illiteracy.

The predecessor of our present superintendent of schools had apparently given no thought to the social relationship of the school to the pupils. The general public, twenty years ago, had no accurate information concerning the schools, and, indeed, seemed to have little interest in them. We heard of flagrant instances of political influence in the selection and promotion of teachers, and later on we had actual knowledge of their humiliation at being forced to obtain through sordid "pull" the positions to which they had a legitimate claim. I had myself once been obliged to enter the saloon of N——, the alderman of our district, to obtain the promise of necessary and long-delayed action on his part for the city's acceptance of the gift of a street fountain, which I had been indirectly instrumental in securing for the neighborhood. I had been informed by his friends that without this attention he would not be likely to act.

Louis set me thinking and opened my mind to many things. Miss Brewster and I decided to keep memoranda of the children we encountered who had been excluded from school for medical reasons, and later our enlarged staff of nurses became equally interested in obtaining data regarding them. When one of the nurses found a small boy attending school while desquamating from scarlet fever, and, Tom Sawyer-like, pulling off the skin to startle his little classmates, we exhibited him to the President of the Department of Health, and I then learned that the possibility of having physicians inspect the school children was under discussion, and that such evidence of its need as we could produce would be helpful in securing an appropriation for this purpose.

I had come to the conclusion that the nurse would be an essential factor in making effec-

tive whatever treatment might be suggested for
the pupils, and, following an observation of
mine to this effect, the president asked me to
take part, as nurse, in the medical supervision
in the schools. This offer it did not seem wise
to accept. We were embarking upon ventures
of our own which would require all our facul-

ties and all our strength. It seemed better
to be free from connections which would make
demand upon our energies for routine work
outside the settlement. Moreover, the time did
not seem ripe for advocating the introduction
of both the doctor and the nurse. The doctor
himself, in this capacity, was an innovation.
The appointment of a nurse would have been
a radical departure.

In 1897 the Department of Health appointed
the first doctors; one hundred and fifty were
assigned to the schools for one hour a day at

a salary of $30 a month. They were expected to examine for contagious diseases and to send out of the classrooms all those who showed suspicious symptoms. It proved to be a perfunctory service and only superficially touched the needs of the children.

In 1902, when a reform administration came into power, the medical staff was reduced and the salary increased to $100 a month, while three hours a day were demanded from the doctors. The Health Commissioner of that administration, an intelligent friend of children, now ordered an examination of all the public school pupils, and New York was horrified to learn of the prevalence of trachoma. Thousands of children were sent out of the schools because of this infectious eye trouble, and in our neighborhood we watched many of them, after school hours, playing with the children for whose protection they had been excluded from the classrooms. Few received treatment, and it followed that truancy was encouraged, and, where medical inspection was most thorough, the classrooms were depleted.

The President of the Department of Education and the Health Commissioner sought for guidance in this predicament. Examination by physicians with the object of excluding children from the classrooms had proved a doubtful blessing. The time had come when it seemed right to urge the addition of the nurse's service to that of the doctor. My colleagues and I offered to show that with her assistance few children would lose their valuable school time and that it would be possible to bring under treatment those who needed it. Reluctant lest the democracy of the school should be invaded by even the most socially minded philanthropy, I exacted a promise from several of the city officials that if the experiment were successful they would use their influence to have the nurse, like the doctor, paid from public funds.

Four schools from which there had been the greatest number of exclusions for medical causes were selected, and an experienced nurse, who possessed tact and initiative, was chosen from the settlement staff to make the demonstration. A routine was devised, and the examining physician sent daily to the nurse all the pupils who were found to be in need of attention, using a code of symbols in order that the children might be spared the chagrin of having diseases due to uncleanliness advertised to their associates.

With the equipment of the settlement bag and, in some of the schools, with no more than the ledge of a window or the corner of a room for the nurse's office, the present system of thorough medical inspection in the schools and of home visiting was inaugurated. Many of the children needed only disinfectant treatment of the eyes, collodion applied to ringworm, or instruction as to cleanliness, and such were returned at once to the class with a minimum loss of precious school time. Where more serious conditions existed the nurse called at the home, explained to the mother what the doctor advised, and, where there was a family physician, urged that the child should be taken to him. In the families of the poor information as to dispensaries was given, and where the mother was at work, and there was no one free to take the child to the dispensary, the nurse herself did this. Where children were sent to the nurse because of uncleanliness, the mother was given tactful instruction and, when necessary, a practical demonstration on the child himself.

One month's trial proved that, with the exception of the very small proportion of major contagious and infectious diseases, the addition of the nurse to the staff made it possible to reverse the object of medical inspection from excluding the children from school to keeping the children in the classroom and under treatment. An enlightened Board of Estimate and

A Short Cut over the Roofs of the Tenements

Apportionment voted $30,000 for the employ-
ment of trained nurses, the first municipalized
school nurses in the world, now a feature of
medical school supervision in many communities in this country and in Europe.

The first nurse was placed on the city pay-
roll in October, 1902, and this marked the beginning of an extraordinary development of the
public control of the physical condition of children. Out of this innovation New York City's
Bureau of Child Hygiene has grown.

The Department of Health now employs 650
nurses for its hospital and preventive work.
Of this number 374, in the year 1914, were
engaged for the Bureau of Child Hygiene.

Poor Louis, who all unconsciously had
started the train of incidents that led to this
practical reform, has long since moved from
his Hester Street home to Kansas, and was
able to write us, as he did with enthusiasm,
of his identification with the West.

Our first expenditures were for " sputum cups
and disinfectants for tuberculosis patients."
The textbooks had said that Jews were practically immune from this disease, and here we
found ourselves in a dense colony of the race
with signs everywhere of the white plague,

which we soon thought it fitting to name
" tailors' disease."

Long before the great work was started by
the municipality to combat its ravages through
education and home visitation, we organized
for ourselves a system of care and instruction
for patients and their families, and wrote to the
institutions that were known to care for tuberculosis cases for the addresses of discharged
patients, that we might call upon them to leave
the cups and disinfectants and instruct the families.

Since 1904 the anti-tuberculosis movement
has been greatly accelerated, and although it is
pre-eminently a disease of poverty and can
never be successfully combated without dealing
with its underlying economic causes—bad
housing, bad workshops, undernourishment,
and so on—the most immediate attack lies in
education in personal hygiene. For this the
approach to the families through the nurse and
her ability to apply scientific truth to the problems of human living have been found to be
invaluable.[1]

Infant mortality is also a social disease—

[1] The National Association for the Study and Prevention of
Tuberculosis in its report for 1915 states that the tuberculosis death
rate in the registration area of the United States has declined from
167.7 in 1905 to 127.7 in 1913 per 100,000 population ; a net saving to
this country of over 200,000 lives from this one disease.

"poverty and ignorance, the twin roots from which this evil springs." There is a large measure of preventable ignorance, and in the efforts for the reduction of infant mortality the intelligent reaction of the tenement-house mother has been re-markably evidenced. In the last analysis babies of the poor are kept alive through the intelligence of the mothers. Pasteurized or modified milk in immaculate contain-ers is of limited value if exposed to pollu-tion in the home, or if it is fed improperly and at irregular periods.

The need of giving the mother training seemed so evident that, in the course of lessons given on the East Side antedating our nursing service, I had demonstrated with a primitive sterilizer a simple method of insuring " safe " milk for babies.

The settlement established a milk station in 1903, when one of its directors began sending milk of high grade from his private dairy. Fol-lowing our principle of building up the homes wherever possible, the modification of the milk has always been taught there. The nurses report that it is very rare to find a woman who cannot learn the lesson when made to understand its importance to her children.

Children under two years who show the greatest need are given the preference in admission to our clinic.  Excellent physicians practicing in the neighborhood have contributed their services as consultants, and conferences are held regularly. In 1914 the number of infants cared for was 518 and the mortality 1.8 per cent. The previous year, with 400 infants, the mortality was one-half of one per cent.

The Health Commissioner of Rochester, N. Y., a pioneer in his specialty, founded municipal milk stations for that city in 1897. He states that the reduction of infant mortality that followed the establishment of the stations was due, not so much to the milk, but to the education that went out with the milk through the nurse and in the press.

In 1911 New York City authorized the municipalization of fifteen milk stations, and so satisfactory was the result that the next year the appropriation permitted more than the trebling of this number. A nurse is attached to each station to follow into the homes and there lay the foundation, through education, for hygienic living. A marked reduction in infant mortality has been brought about and, moreover, a realization, on the part of the city, of the immeasurable social and economic value of keeping the babies alive.

The Federal Children's Bureau in its first report on the study of infant mortality in the United States showed that, in the city selected for investigation, the infant death rate, in those sections where conditions were worst, was more than five times that in the choice residential sections.

This report constitutes a serious indictment of society, and should goad civic and social conscience to aggressive action. But there are evidences (and, indeed, the existence of the Bureau is one) that the public is beginning to realize the profound importance in our national life of saving the children that are born.

Perhaps nothing indicates more impressively our contempt for alien customs than the general attitude taken toward the midwife. In other lands she holds a place of respect, but in this country there seems to be a general determination on the part of physicians and departments of health to ignore her existence and leave her free to practice without fit preparation, despite the fact that her services are extensively used in humble homes. In New York City the midwife brings into the world over forty per cent. of all the babies born there, and ninety-eight per cent. of those among the Italians.

We had many experiences with them, beginning with poor Ida, the carpenter's wife, and some that had the salt of humor. Before our first year had passed I wrote to the superintendent of a large relief society operating in our neighborhood, advising that the society discontinue its employment of midwives as a branch of relief, because of their entire lack of standards and their exemption from restraining influence.

To force attention to the harmful effect of leaving the midwife without training in midwifery and asepsis free to attend women in childbirth, the Union Settlement in 1905 financed an investigation under the auspices of a committee of which I was chairman.

A trained nurse was selected to inquire into

and report upon the practice of the midwives. The inquiry disclosed the extent to which habit, tradition, and economic necessity made the midwife practically indispensable, and gave ample proof of the neglect, ignorance, and criminality that prevailed; logical consequences of the policy that had been pursued. The

Commissioner of Health and eminent obstetricians now co-operated to improve matters, and legislation was secured making it mandatory for the Department of Health to regulate the practice of midwifery. Five years later the first school for midwives in America was established in connection with Bellevue Hospital.

Part of the duty assigned to nurses of the Bureau of Child Hygiene is to inspect the bags

of the midwives licensed to practice, and to visit the new-born in the campaign to wipe out *ophthalmia neonatorum,* that tragically frequent and preventable cause of blindness among the new-born.

These are a few of the manifestations of the new era in the development of the nurse's work. She is enlisted in the crusade against disease and for the promotion of right living, beginning even before life itself is brought forth, through infancy into school life, on through adolescence, with its appeal to repair the omissions of the past. Her duties take her into factory and workshop, and she has identified herself with the movement against the premature employment of children, and for the protection of men and women who work that they may not risk health and life itself while earning their living. The nurse is being socialized, made part of a community plan for the communal health. Her contribution to human welfare, unified and harmonized with those powers which aim at care and prevention, rather than at police power and punishment, forms part of the great policy of bringing human beings to a higher level.

With the incorporation of the nurse's service in municipal and state departments for the preservation of health, other agencies, under private and semi-public auspices, have expanded their functions to the sick.

I had felt that the American Red Cross Society held a unique position among its sister societies of other nations, and that in time it might be an agency that could consciously provide valuable " moral equivalents for war." The whole subject, in these troubled times, is revived in my memory, and I find that in 1908 I began to urge that in a country dedicated to peace it would be fitting for the American Red Cross to consecrate its efforts to the upbuilding of life and the prevention of disaster, rather than to emphasize its identification with the ravages of war.

The concrete recommendation made was that the Red Cross should develop a system of visiting nursing in the vast, neglected country areas. The suggestion has been adopted and an excellent beginning made with a Department of Town and Country Nursing directed by a special committee. A generous gift started an endowment for its administration. Many communities not in the registered area and remote from the centers of active social propaganda will be given stimulus to organize for nursing service, and from this other medical and social measures will inevitably grow. It requires no far reach of the imagination to visualize the time when our country will be districted from the northernmost to the southernmost point, with the trained graduate nurse entering the home wherever there is illness, caring for the patient, preaching the gospel of health, and teaching in simplest form the essentials of hygiene. Such an organization of national scope, its powers directed toward raising the standard in the homes without sacrifice of independence, is bound to promote the social progress of the nation.

In the year 1909 the Metropolitan Life Insurance Company undertook the nursing of its industrial policyholders—an important event in the annals of visiting nursing. I had suggested the practicality of this to one of the officials of the company, a man of broad experience, and he, immediately responsive, provided opportunity for me to present to his colleagues evidence of the reduction of mortality, the hastening of convalescence, and the ability to bring to sick people the resources that the community provides for treatment through the institution of visiting nursing.

The company employed our staff to care for its patients, and the experiment has been extended until a nursing service practically covers its industrial policyholders in Canada and the United States. The company thereby gave an enormous impetus to education and hygiene in the homes and treatment of the sick on the only basis that makes it possible for persons of small means to receive nursing without charity—namely, through insurance.

The demand for the public health nurse coming from all sides was so great that for a time it could not be ade- quately met. Women of in- itiative and personality with broad education were needed, for much of the work required pioneering zeal. Instructive inspection, on the nurse's part, like other educational work, requires suitable and sound  preparation, a superstructure of efficiency upon woman's natural aptitudes.

The Henry Street Settlement and other groups with well-established visiting nursing systems responded to the need by offering op- portunities for post-graduate training and ex- perience in the newly opened field of public health nursing, and sought co-ordination with formal educational institutions for instruction in social theories and pedagogy. In 1910 the

Department of Nursing and Health was created at Teachers College, Columbia University, embracing in its completed form the Department of Hospital Economics established there in 1899 by the efforts of training-school superintendents. This department is in affiliation with the settlement. At least four important training-schools for nurses are now working under the direction of universities, and other provision has been made to give education supplementary to the hospital training.

Nurses themselves have taken the initiative in securing the means for equipping women in their profession to meet the new requirements. They are providing helpful literature and finding stimulating associations with others enlisted in similar efforts for human welfare. I had the honor to be elected first president of the National Organization for Public Health Nursing. At the conference held in 1913 (less than a year after the formation of the society) an assemblage of women gathered from all parts of the country to seek guidance and inspiration for this work, and something that was very like religious fervor characterized their meetings.

The need of consecration to the sick and the young that has touched generation after generation with new impulse was manifested in their eagerness to serve the community. From the root of the old gospel another branch has grown, a realization that the call to the nurse is not only for the bedside care of the sick, but to help in seeking out the deep-lying basic causes of illness and misery, that in the future there may be less sickness to nurse and to cure.

A pleasant indication that the academic world reached out its fellowship to the nurses in their zeal for public service was given some months later when Mt. Holyoke College, at the commemoration of its seventy-fifth anniversary, honored me by conferring on me the LL.D. degree.

CHAPTER IV

CHILDREN AND PLAY

THE visitor who sees our neighborhood for the first time at the hour when school is dismissed reacts with joy or dismay to the sight, not paralleled in any part of the world, of thousands of little ones on a single city block.

Out they pour, the little hyphenated Americans, more conscious of their patriotism than perhaps any other large group of children that could be found in our land; unaware that to some of us they carry on their shoulders our hopes of a finer, more democratic America, when the worthy things they bring to us shall be recognized, and the good in their old-world traditions and culture shall be mingled with the best that lies within our new-world ideals. Only through knowledge is one fortified to resist the onslaught of arguments of the superficial observer who, dismayed by the sight, is conscious only of " hordes " and " danger to America " in these little children.

They are irresistible. They open up wide vistas of the many lands from which they come. The multitude passes: swinging walk, lagging step; smiling, serious—just little children, forever appealing, and these, perhaps,

more than others, stir the emotions. "Crime, ignorance, dirt, anarchy!" Not theirs the fault if any of these be true, although sometimes perfectly good children are spoiled, as Jacob Riis, that buoyant lover of them, has said. As a nation we must rise or fall as we serve or fail these future citizens.

Their appeal suggests that social exclusions and prejudices separate far more effectively than distance and differing language. They bring a hope that a better relationship—even the great brotherhood—is not impossible, and

that through love and understanding we shall come to know the shame of prejudice.

Instinctively the sympathetic observer feels the possibilities of the young life that passes before the settlement doors, and sincerity demands that something shall be known of the conditions, economic, political, religious, or, perchance, of the mere spirit of venture that brought them here. How often have the conventionally educated been driven to the library to obtain that historic perspective of the people

who are in our midst, without which they cannot be understood! What fascinating excursions have been made into folklore in the effort
to comprehend some strange custom unexpect-
edly encountered!

When the anxious friends of the dying Italian brought a chicken to be killed over him,
the tenement-house bed became the sacrificial
altar of long ago; and when the old, rabbinical-
looking grandfather took
hairs from the head of
the sick child, a bit of
his finger-nail, and a
garment that had been
close to his body, and
cast them into the
river while he devoutly
prayed that the little

life might be spared, he declared his faith in
the purification of running water.

It is necessary to spend a summer in our
neighborhood to realize fully the conditions
under which many thousands of children are
reared. One night during my first month on
the East Side, sleepless because of the heat, I
leaned out of the window and looked down on
Rivington Street. Life was in full course there.
Some of the push-cart venders still sold their
wares. Sitting on the curb directly under my

window, with her feet in the gutter, was a woman, drooping from exhaustion, a baby at her breast. The fire-escapes, considered the most desirable sleeping-places, were crowded with the youngest and the oldest; children were asleep on the sidewalks, on the steps of

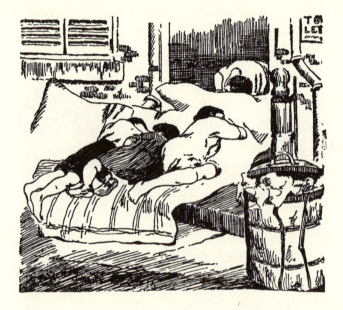

the houses and in the empty push-carts; some of the more venturesome men and women with mattress or pillow staggered toward the river-front or the parks. I looked at my watch. It was two o'clock in the morning!

Many times since that summer of 1893 have I seen similar sights, and always I have been impressed with the kindness and patience, sometimes the fortitude, of our neighbors, and I

have marveled that out of conditions distress-
ing and nerve-destroying as these so many
children have emerged into fine manhood and
womanhood, and often, because of their early
experiences, have become intelligent factors in
promoting measures to guard the next generation against conditions which they know to be
destructive.

Before I lived in the midst of this dense child
population, and while I was still in the hospital,
I had been touched by glimpses of the life revealed in the games played in the children's
ward. Up to that time my knowledge of little
ones had been limited to those to whom the
people in fairy tales were real, and whose games
and stories reflected the protective care of their
elders. My own earliest recollections of play
had been of story-telling, of housekeeping with
all the things in miniature that grown-ups use,
and of awed admiration of the big brother who
graciously permitted us to witness hair-raising
performances in the barn, to which we paid admittance in pins. The children in the hospital
ward who were able to be about, usually on
crutches or with arms in slings, played "Ambulance" and the "Gerry Society." The latter
game dramatized their conception of the famous
Society for the Prevention of Cruelty to Children as an ogre that would catch them. The

ambulance game was of a child, or a man at work, injured and carried away to the hospital.

Many years' familiarity with the children's attempts to play in the streets has not made me indifferent to its pathos, which is not the less real because the children themselves are unconscious of it. In the midst of the push-cart market, with its noise, confusion, and jostling, the checker or crokinole board is precariously perched on the top of a hydrant, constantly knocked over by the crowd and patiently replaced by the little children. One tearful small boy described his morning when he said he had done nothing but play, but first the " cop " had snatched his dice, then his " cat " (a piece of wood sharpened at both ends), and nobody wanted him to chalk on the sidewalk, and he had been arrested for throwing a ball.

A man since risen to distinction in educational circles, whose childhood was passed in our neighborhood, told me how he and his companions had once taken a dressmaker's lay figure. They had no money to spend on the theater and no place to play in but a cellar. They had admired the gaudy posters of a melodrama in which the hero rescues the lady and carries her over a chasm. Having no lady in their cast, they borrowed the dressmaker's lay figure—without permission. Fortunately, and accidentally, they escaped detection. It is not difficult to see how the entire course of this boy's career might have been altered if arrest had followed, with its consequent humiliation and degradation. At least, looking back upon it, the young man sees how the incident might have deflected his life.

The instruction in folk-dancing which the children now receive in the public schools and recreation centers has done much to develop a wholesome and delightful form of exercise, and has given picturesqueness to the dancing in the streets. But yesterday I found myself pausing on East Houston Street to watch a group of children assemble at the sound of a familiar dance from a hurdy-gurdy, and looking up I met the sympathetic smile of a teamster who also had stopped. The children, absorbed in their dance, were quite unconscious that congested traffic had halted and that busy people had taken a moment from their engrossing problems to be refreshed by the sight of their youth and grace. For that brief instant even the cry of " War Extra " was unheeded.

Touching as are the little children deprived of opportunity for wholesome play, a deeper compassion stirred our hearts when we began to realize the critically tender age at which many of them share the experiences, anxieties, and tragedies of the adult. I cannot efface from my memory the picture of a little eight-year-old girl whom I once found standing on a chair to reach a washtub, trying with her tiny hands to cleanse some bed-linen which would have been a task for an older person. Every few minutes the child got down from her chair to peer into the next room where her mother and the new-born baby lay, all her little mind intent upon giving relief and comfort. She had been alone with her mother when the baby was born and terror was on her face.

I think the memory never left her, but it may be only that her presence called up, even after the lapse of years, a vision of the anxious little face inevitably contrasted in my mind with the picture of irresponsible childhood.

At about the same time we made the acquaintance of the K—— family, through nursing one of the children. The mother was a large-framed, phlegmatic, seemingly emotionless type, although she did show appreciation of our liking for her children. The father was only occasionally mentioned. We assumed that he was away seeking work, a common explanation then of the absence of the men of the families. One afternoon I stopped at their house to make arrangements for the children's trip to the country. Early the next morning, awakened by a pounding on the door, I opened it to find little Esther beside herself with excitement, repeating over and over, " My mother she die! My mother she die!" Following fast, it was not possible to keep pace with her. When, breathless, I entered their rooms it was to see the mother's body hanging from a doorway. She had been brooding over a summons to testify in court that morning against her husband, who had been arrested for bigamy, and this was her answer to the court and to the other woman.

The frightened little children were scattered among different institutions. From one of these Esther was sent West, to a home that was found for her. Possibly she was so young that the terrible picture faded from her mind. At least there was no mention of it in the first letter which she wrote, announcing that her new home was a farm and that they had " six cows, eighty chickens, eleven pigs, and a *nephew.*" The nephew Esther eventually married.

In the first party of children that we sent to the country were three little girls, daughters of a skilled cobbler. The mother, a complaining, exacting invalid, spent a large proportion of her husband's earnings for patent medicines. Annie,

not quite twelve, was the household drudge,
and the coming of the settlement nurse lifted
only part of her burden. The new friends, determined to get at least two weeks of care-free
childhood for the little girls, procured an invitation for them, through a Fresh-Air agency,
from a farmer in the western part of the state.
It was necessary to secure the mother's admission to a hospital during the time the children
would be absent from home—not an easy task,
as she was not what is termed a " hospital
case." When we met the children at the railroad
station on their return, their joyousness and
bubbling spirits attracted the attention of the on-
lookers; but as Annie neared home its responsibilities fell like a heavy cloud upon her, and
before we reached the tenement she was silent.
Her quick eye discerned the absence of the
brick which had kept the front hall door open,
and in a second she had darted into the yard
and replaced it. Before we left, with sleeves
rolled up she was beginning to wash the pile
of dishes that had accumulated in her absence.
Gone was the gayety. The little drudge had
resumed her place. Later, when the child swore
falsely to her age, and the notary public, upon
whose certificate employment papers could at
that time be obtained, affixed his signature to
her perjury, the position she secured as cash

girl in the basement of a department store was, to her, emancipation from hateful labor and an opportunity for fellowship with children.

Recalling early days, I am constantly reminded of the sympathy and comprehension of those friends who, though not stimulated as my comrade and I were by constant reminders of the children's needs, from the beginning promoted and often anticipated our efforts to provide innocent recreation. We had not thought of the possibility of giving pleasure to large groups of children in picnics and day parties, when a friend, a few days after our arrival in the neighborhood, asked us to celebrate his sister's birthday by giving " fun " to some of our new acquaintances. I yet remember the thrill I felt when I realized that this gift was not for shoes or practical necessities, but for " just what children anywhere would like."

Two memories of this first party stand out sharply: the songs the children sang,—" She's More to be Pitied than Censured," and " Judge, Forgive Him, 'Tis His First Offense,"—painfully revealing a precocious knowledge, and their ecstasy at the sight of a wonderful dogwood tree. Now, when the settlement children go on day parties, they have another repertory, and the music they learn in the public schools reflects the finer thought for the child.

During the two years that Miss Brewster and I lived in the Jefferson Street house we frequently made up impromptu parties to visit the distant parks, usually on Sunday afternoons when we were likely to be free. After a while it was not difficult to secure comradeship for

the children from men and women of our acquaintance, and the parties were multiplied. In the winter, rumors of " a fine hill all covered with snow " on Riverside Drive would be a stimulus to secure a sled or improvise a toboggan, and we found that, given opportunity and encouragement, the city tenement boys threw themselves readily into venturesome sport.

Happily some of the early prejudice against ball-playing on Sunday has vanished. We were perplexed in those days to explain to the lads why, when they saw the ferries and trains convey golfers suitably attired and expensively

And their Ecstasy at the Sight of a Wonderful
Dogwood Tree

equipped for a day's sport, their own games should outrage respectable citizens and cause them to be constantly "chased" by the police. The saloons could be entered, as everybody knew, and I remember a father, defending his eight-year-old son from an accusation of theft, instancing as proof of the child's trustworthiness that "all the Christians on Jackson Street sent him for their beer on Sundays."

In our search for a place where the boys might play undisturbed, one of the settlement residents, a never-failing friend of the young people, invoked the Federal Government itself, and secured for them an unused field on Governor's Island.

Now, in summer time, many of the organized activities of the settlement are removed from the neighborhood. Early in the season the "hikers" begin their walks with club leaders. I felt a glow of happiness one Sunday morning when I stood on the steps of our house and watched six different groups of boys set off for the country, with ball and bat and sandwiches, each group led by a young man who had himself been a member of our early parties and had been first introduced to trees and open spaces, and the more active forms of healthful play by his settlement friends.

The woeful lack of imagination displayed in

building a city without recognizing the need of
its citizens for recreation through play, music,
and art, has been borne in upon us many times.
New Yorkers need to be reminded that the
Metropolitan Museum of Art was effectually
closed to a large proportion of the citizens until,
on May 31, 1891, it opened its doors on Sundays. It is interesting to recall that of the
80,000 signatures to the petition for this privilege, 50,000 were of residents of the lower East
Side and were presented by the " Working People's Petition Committee." The report of the
Museum trustees following the Sunday opening notes that after a little disorder and confusion at the start the experiment proved a success; that the attendance was " respectable, law-
abiding, and intelligent," and that " the laboring classes were well represented." They were

also obliged to report, however, that the Sunday opening had "offended some of the Museum's best friends and supporters," and that it had "resulted in the loss of a bequest of $50,000."

When we left the tenement house we were fortunate to find for sale, on a street that still bore evidences of its bygone social glory, a house which readily lent itself to the restorer's touch. Tradition says that many of these fine old East Side houses were built by cabinet-makers who came over from England during the War of 1812 and remained here as citizens. The generous purchaser allowed us freedom to repair, restore, and alter, as our taste directed. Attractive as we found the house, we were even more excited over the possibilities of the little back yard. Our first organized effort for the neighborhood was to convert this yard and one belonging to an adjacent school, with, later, the yard of a third house rented by one of our residents, into a miniature but very complete playground. There was so little precedent to guide us that our resourcefulness was stimulated, and we succeeded in achieving what the President of the National Playground Association has called the "Bunker Hill" of playgrounds.

Along the borders we planted bright-colored flowers—which were not disturbed by the children. An old wistaria vine on a trellis covered nearly a third of the playground, and two ailanthus trees, usually regarded with contempt by tree lovers, were highly cherished by those who otherwise would have lived a treeless life. Window-boxes jutted from the rear windows of the two houses controlled by the settlement, and in one corner, shaded by a striped awning, we put the big sand-pile. Joy-giving "scups" (the local name for swings) were erected, and some suitable gymnastic apparatus, parallel bars and overhead ladder placed. Baby hammocks were swung, their occupants tenderly cared for by little mothers and little fathers. Manual training was provided by a picturesque sailor from Sailors' Snug Harbor, who, at a stretching frame, taught the making of hammocks.

In the morning under the pergola an informal kindergarten was conducted, and in the afternoon attendants directed play and taught the use of gymnastic apparatus. Later in the day the mothers and older children came, and a little hurdy-gurdy occasionally marked the rhythm of the dance. So interested in the playground were the household and their visitors that at odd moments an enthusiast would rush in from other duties and give the hurdy-gurdy

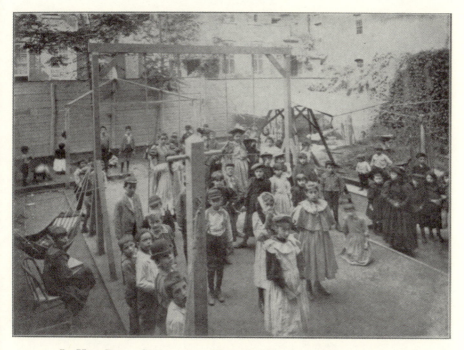

It Has Been Called the "Bunker Hill" of Playgrounds

The Children Play on Our Roof

an extra turn, to supplement the entertainment. At night the baby hammocks and chairs were stored away and Japanese lanterns illuminated the playground, which then welcomed the young people who, after their day's work, took pleasure in each other's society and in singing familiar songs.

On Saturday afternoons the playground was used almost exclusively by fathers and mothers, but it was a pretty sight at all times, and the value placed upon it by those who used it was far in excess of our own estimate. It was something more than amusement that moved us when a young couple, who had been invited to one of the evening parties, stood at the back door of the settlement house and gazed admiringly at the little pleasure place. Gowned in white, we awaited our guests, and as I rose from the bench under the pergola to cross the yard and give them welcome, the young printer said with enthusiasm, " This must be like the scenes of country life in English novels."

It was a heaven of delight to the children, and ingenuity was displayed by those who sought admittance. The children soon learned that " little mothers " and their charges had precedence, and there was rivalry as to who should hold the family baby. When (as rarely happened) there was none in the family, a baby was borrowed. Six-year-olds, clasping babies of stature almost equal to their own, would stand outside, hoping to attract attention to their special claims. Once, when the playground was filled to capacity, and the sidewalk in front of the house was thronged, the Olympian at the gate endeavored to make it clear that no more could enter. One persistent small girl stood stolidly and when reminded of the condition said, " Yes, teacher, but can't I get in? I ain't got no mother."

There was much illness, unemployment, and consequent suffering the next winter. One day, when I visited a school in the neighborhood, the principal asked the pupils if they knew me. She doubtless anticipated some reference to the material services which the settlement had rendered, but the answer to her question was a glad chorus of, " Yes, ma'am, yes, ma'am, she's our scupping teacher." " Teacher " was a generic term for the residents, and nothing that the settlement had contributed to the life of the neighborhood impressed the children as had the playground. It is worth reminding those who are associated with young people that the power to influence is given to those who play with, rather than to those who only teach, them. Our children on the East Side are not peculiar in this respect. To this day I receive letters from men and women who try to recall themselves to my memory by saying that they once played in our back yard.

An organized propaganda for outdoor gymnasia and playgrounds crystallized in 1898 in the formation of the Outdoor Recreation League,

in which the settlement participated. The tireless president of the League eventually succeeded in obtaining the use of a large space in our neighborhood, originally purchased by the city, during a brief reform administration, for a park. Some very undesirable tenement houses had been destroyed, and when a Tammany administration returned to power a hot summer was allowed to pass with nothing done to accomplish the original purpose. Unsightly holes, once cellars, remained to fill with stagnant water, amputated sewer- and gas-pipes were exposed, and among these the children played mimic battles of the Spanish-American War, then in progress.

The accident that the Commissioner of Health, a semi-invalid, felt gratitude to a trained nurse who had cared for him, gave me an opportunity to approach him on the subject. He promised (and he kept his promise) to use his influence to get an appropriation on the score of the menace to the health of the city. The appropriation was sufficient to fill in the space and surround it with a fence, and the Outdoor Recreation League was able to demonstrate the value of playgrounds. In 1902 the Board of Estimate and Apportionment of Mayor Seth Low's reform administration, at its first meeting, appropriated money for the equipment and maintenance of Seward Park, as it was named,—the first municipal playground in New York City. So much interest had been aroused in this phase of city government that two city officials left the board meeting while it was in progress to telephone to the settlement that the appropriation had been passed.

Many friends of the children combined to urge the use of the public schools as recreation centers, and in the summer of 1898 the first schools were opened for that purpose. Those of us who had practical experience helped to start these by acting as volunteer inspectors. The settlement then felt justified in devoting less effort to its own playground, and deflected some of the energies it required to meet other pressing needs.

It is a delight to give the children stories from the Bible and the old mythologies, fairy tales, and lives of heroes, and we mark as epochal Maude Adams's inspiration to invite our children and others not likely to have the opportunity to see Peter Pan. She has given joy to thousands, but it is doubtful if she can measure, as we do, the influence of " the everlasting boy." Through him romance has touched these children, and not a few of the letters spontaneously written to Peter Pan from tenement homes have seemed to us not unworthy of Barrie himself. Protest against leaving the big, familiar farmhouse at one of our country places, when an overflow of visitors necessitated a division of the little ones at night, was immediately withdrawn when the children were told that the annex, perched on high ground, was a " Wendy House."

The need of care for convalescents was early recognized, and the settlement's first country house was for them. It was opened in 1899, and its maintenance is the generous gift of a young woman, a member of the early group that gathered in the Henry Street house. We soon felt, however, that it was essential that children and young people as well as invalids should have knowledge of life other than that of the crowded tenement and factory; and from the time of the establishment of our first kindergarten we longed to have the children know the reality of the things they sang about, the birds and animals which so often formed the subject of their games. A little girl in one of the parties taken to see Peter Pan turned to her beloved club leader when the crocodile appeared and asked timidly if it was a *field-mouse!* A recent lesson had been about that " animal." It

seems almost incredible that the description, probably supplemented by a picture, should not have made a more definite impression upon the child's mind; but I am inclined to think that little children can form no accurate conception of unknown objects from pictures or description. A neighborhood teacher took her class to the menagerie in Central Park just after a lesson on the cow and its " gifts "—milk, cream, butter. She hoped that the young buffalo's resemblance to the cow might suggest itself to the children who, of course, had never seen a cow. In answer to her question an eager little boy gave testimony to the impression the lesson had made on his mind when he answered, " Yes, ma'am. I know it. It's a *butterfly*."

We value the " day parties " for incidental education as well as for the pleasure they afford. Each year as spring approaches a census is taken of the surrounding blocks, that the new arrivals may be included in the excursions. The most treasured invitations for these parties come from friends whose country estates are near enough to offer hospitality, and to whose gardens and stables the children are taken. The larger parties, composed of women and children, usually go to the seashore in chartered cars, and these excursions, purely recreative, compete, and not unsuccessfully, with the clambakes and outings of the old-time political leaders.

The beautiful country places presented to the settlement for vacation purposes, and the comparative readiness with which money for equipment and maintenance for non-paying guests has been given, indicates the favor with which this development of neighborhood work is regarded. Opportunities for confidence and mutual understanding, not always possible in the formal relationships of clubs and classes, are afforded by the intimacy of country-house

The Kindergarten Children Learn the Reality of the Things They Sing About

parties. The possibility of giving direction at critical periods of character-formation, particularly during adolescence, and of discovering clews to deep-lying causes of disturbance, makes the country life a valuable extension of the organized social work of the settlement. " Riverholm," overhanging the Hudson; " Camp Henry," on a beautiful lake; the " House in the

Woods," " Echo Hill Farm," and a commodious house in New Jersey, lent by friends during the summer months, give us the means whereby some of the plans we cherish may be carried out.

It would be inconsistent with settlement theories if these country places did not express refinement and beauty,—the beauty that belongs to simplicity,—not only in the buildings, but

also in the service and housekeeping. It has
seemed to us, therefore, worth the additional
expenditure of effort to have small, distinct
household units wherever practicable. People
who live in crowded homes, walk on crowded
streets, ride on crowded cars, and as children
attend crowded classrooms, must inevitably ac-

"House in the Woods."

quire distorted views of life; and the settlement is reluctant to add to these the experience
of crowded country life. Valuable training in
housekeeping is possible in a household even
of from fifteen to twenty-five persons,—a small
unit according to New York standards,—and
tactful direction can often be given toward ac-

quiring those manners generally recognized as
"good." Many of the children who come to
us know only foreign customs and foreign table-
manners; and the extreme difficulty of maintain-

ing orderly home life in the tenement makes
it important to supplement the home-training
or to supply what it can never give. Indeed,
we recognize in this desire to protect our children from being marked as peculiar or alien
because of non-essential differences the same
reason that urges the careful mother to insist

on "manners," that her children may not be discredited when they mingle with the fastidious.

The ideal of limitation as to numbers cannot always be carried out, and naturally it does not apply to the camp, where a freer and less conventional life attracts and satisfies boys and young men.

The older members of the settlement, who are earning money, use the camp and country places as clubs, paying for the privilege and conforming to the regulations which they have had a share in establishing.

Those who have promoted the various Fresh-Air agencies throughout the country may not realize that physical benefit is not all that has

been secured. We are persuaded that opportunity to know life away from the city is in part the explanation of the increasing number of city boys who elect training in agriculture and forestry. Formerly, when careers were discussed, the future held no happiness unless it promised a profession—law or medicine.

If I appear to lay too much stress upon the importance of play and recreation, it may be well to point out that it is one way of recognizing the dignity of the child. The study of juvenile delinquency shows how often the young offender's presence in the courts may be traced to a play-impulse for which there was no safe outlet.

Perhaps nothing more definitely indicates the changed attitude toward children and play than the fact that last summer (1914) the police officers of the precinct called to enlist our co-operation in carrying out the orders of the city administration that during certain hours of the day traffic was to be shut off from designated streets, that the children might play there. The visit brought to mind years of painstaking effort to secure the toleration of harmless play, and the hope we had dared to express, despite incredulity on the part of the police, that some day the children might come to regard them as guardians and protectors, rather than as a fear-inspiring and hated force. One captain of the precinct, at least, had proved the practicability of our theory, and when he was transferred we lost a valuable co-worker. The Governor of New York, campaigning for re-election in the fall of this year (1914), advocated that public schools should be surrounded by playgrounds at "no matter what cost."

Tremendous impetus has been given to the playground movement throughout the entire country by individuals and societies organized for the purpose. Wise men and women have expounded the social philosophy of play and recreation, pointing out that these may afford wholesome expression for energies which might otherwise be diverted into channels disastrous to peace and happiness; that clean sport and stimulating competition can replace the gang feud and even modify racial antagonisms. The most satisfactory evidence of this conviction is, of course, the recognition of the child's right to play, as an integral part of his claim upon the state.

CHAPTER V

EDUCATION AND THE CHILD

PERHAPS nothing makes a profounder impression on the newcomer to our end of the city than the value placed by the Jew upon education; an overvaluation, one is tempted to think, in view of the sacrifices which are made, particularly for the boys,—though of late years the girls' claims have penetrated even to the Oriental home.

One afternoon a group of old-world women sat in the reception-room at the settlement while one of the residents sang and played negro melodies. With the melancholy minor of " Let My People Go," the women began crooning a song that told the story of Cain and Abel. The melody was not identical, but so similar that they thought they recognized the song as their own; and when a discussion arose upon the coincidence that two persecuted peoples should claim this melody, the women, touched by the music, confessed their homesick longing for Russia—for Russia that had dealt so unkindly with them.

"Rather a stone for a pillow in my own home," said one woman on whom life had pressed hard. "Would you go back?" she was asked. "Oh, no, no, no!" emphasizing the

words by a swaying of the body and a shaking of the head. "It is not poverty we fear. It is not money we are seeking here. We do not expect things for ourselves. It is the chance for the children, education and freedom for them."

The passion of the Russian Jews for intellectual attainment recalls the spirit of the early New England families and their willingness to forego every comfort that a son might be set apart for the ministry. Here we are often witnesses of long-continued deprivation on the part of every member of the family, a willingness to deny themselves everything but the barest necessities of life, that there may be a doctor, a lawyer, or a teacher among them. Submission to bad housing, excessive hours, and poor working conditions is defended as of " no matter because the children will have better and can go to school—maybe college." Said a baker who showed the ill-effects of basement and night work and whose three rooms housed a family of ten: " My boy is already in the high school. If I can't keep on, the Herr Gott will take it up where I leave off."

A painful instance was that of a woman who came to the settlement one evening. Her son was studying music under one of the most famous masters in Vienna, and she had exiled herself to New York in order to earn more money for him than she could possibly earn at home. Literally, as I afterwards discovered, she spent nothing upon herself. A tenement family gave her lodging (a bed on chairs) and food, in return for scrubbing done after her day's work in the necktie factory. The Viennese master, not knowing his pupil's circumstances, or, it is possible, not caring, had written that the young man needed to give a concert, an additional demand which it was utterly impossible for her to meet. She had already given up her home, she had relinquished her wardrobe, and she had sold her grave for him.

One young lad stands out among the many who came to talk over their desire to go through college. He dreamed of being great and, this period of hardship over, of placing his family in comfort. I felt it right to emphasize his obligation to the family; the father was dead, the mother burdened with anxiety for the numerous children. How reluctant I was to do this he could not realize; only fourteen, he had impressed us with his fine courage and intelligence, and it was hard to resist the young pleader and to analyze with him the commonplace sordid facts. He had planned to work all summer, to work at night, and he was hardly going to eat at all. But his young mind grasped, almost before I had finished, the ethical importance of meeting his nearest duties. He has met the family claims with generosity, and has realized all our expectations for him by acquiring through his own efforts education and culture; and he evinces an unusual sense of civic responsibility.

Those who have had for many years continuous acquaintance with the neighborhood have countless occasions to rejoice at the good use made of the education so ardently desired, and

achieved in spite of what have seemed over-
whelming odds. New York City is richer for
the contributions made to its civic and educational life by the young people who grew up
in and with the settlements, and who are not
infrequently ready crusaders in social causes.
A country gentleman one day lamented to me
that he had failed to keep in touch with what
he was pleased to call our humanitarian zeal,
and recalled his own early attempt to take an
East Side boy to his estate and employ him.
" He could not even learn to harness a horse!"
he said, with implied contempt of such unfath-
omable inefficiency. Something he said of the
lad's characteristics made it possible for me to
identify him, and I was able to add to that unsatisfactory first chapter another, which told of
the boy's continuance in school, of his success
as a teacher in one of the higher institutions
of learning, and of his remarkable intelligence
in certain vexed industrial problems.

Such achievements are the more remarkable
because the restricted tenement home, where the
family life goes on in two or three rooms,
affords little opportunity for reading or study.
A vivid picture of its limitations was presented
by the boy who sought a quiet corner in a busy
settlement. "I can never study at home," he

said, " because sister is always using the table
to wash the dishes."

Study-rooms were opened in the settlement in
1907, where the boys and girls find, not only
a quiet, restful place in which to do their work,
but also the needed " coaching." The school
work is supplemented by illuminating bulletins
on current topics, and the young student is provided with the aid which in other conditions is
given by parents or older brothers and sisters.
Such study-rooms are now maintained by the
Board of Education in numerous schools of the
city,—" Thanks to the example set by the settlement," the superintendent of the New York
school system reported.

The settlement children are given instruction
in the selection of books before they are old
enough to take out their cards in the public
libraries. Once a week, on Friday afternoon,
when there are no lessons to be prepared, our
study-room is reserved for these smallest
readers. The books are selected with reference
to their tastes and attainments, and fairy tales
are on the shelves in great numbers. Of course,
no settlement could entirely satisfy the insa-
tiable desire for these.

One day when the room was being used for
study purposes a wee neighbor sauntered in and
said to the custodian, " Please, I'd like a fairy

tale." Although reminded that these books were not given out excepting on the special day, the child lingered. She saw a boy's request for "The Life of Alexander Hamilton" and a girl's wish for "The Life of Joan of Arc" complied with. Evidently there was a way to get one's heart's desire. The child went

out, reappeared in a few moments, and with an air of confidence again addressed the librarian, this time with, *"Please, I'd like the life of a giant."*

It is easy to excite sympathy in our neighborhood for people deprived of books and learning. One year I accompanied a party of Northern people to the Southern Educational Conference. We were all much stirred by the appeal of an itinerant Southern minister who told how the poor white natives traveled miles over the mountains to hear books read. He pictured vividly the deprivation of his neighbors, who had no access to libraries of any kind. When I returned to the settlement and related the story to the young people in the clubs, without suggestion on my part they eagerly voted to send the minister books to form a library; and for two years or more, until the Southerner wrote that he had sufficient for his purpose, the clubs purchased from their several funds one book each month, suited to different ages and tastes, according to their own excellent discrimination.

The first public school established in New York City (Number 1) is on Henry Street. Number 2 is a short distance from it, on the same street, and Number 147 is at our corner. Between their sites are several semi-public and private educational institutions, and from School No. 1 to School No. 147 the distance is not more than three-quarters of a mile.

It is not unnatural, therefore, that the school should loom large in our consciousness of the life of the child. The settlement at no time would, even if it could, usurp the place of school or home. It seeks to work with both or to supplement either. The fact that it is

flexible and is not committed to any fixed programme gives opportunity for experimentation
not possible in a rigid system, and the results
of these experiments must have affected school
methods, at least in New York City.

Intelligent social workers seize opportunities
for observation, and almost unconsciously develop methods to meet needs. They see condi-

tions as they are, and become critical of systems
as they act and react upon the child or fail to
reach him at all. They reverse the method of
the school teacher, who approaches the child
with preconceived theories and a determination
to work them out. Where the school fails, it
appears to the social workers to do so because
it makes education a thing apart,—because it
separates its work from all that makes up the
child's life outside the classroom. Great emphasis is now laid upon the oversight of the
physical condition of children from the time of
their birth through school life; but the sugges-

tion of this extension of socialized parental control did not emanate from those within the school system.

Cooking has been taught in the public schools for many years, and the instruction is of great value to those who are admitted to the classes; but appropriations have never been sufficient to meet all the requirements, and the teaching is given in grades already depleted by the girls who have gone to work, and who will perhaps never again have leisure or inclination to  learn how to prepare meals for husband and children,—the most important business in life for most women.

The laboratory method employed in the schools never seemed to us sufficiently related to the home conditions of vast numbers of the city's population; and, therefore, when the settlement undertook, according to its theory, to supplement the girls' education, all the essentials of our own housekeeping—stove, refrigerator, bedrooms, and so on—were utilized. But neither were single bedrooms and rooms set apart for distinct purposes entirely satisfactory in teaching domestic procedure to the average neighbor; and the leader finally developed out of her knowledge of their home conditions the admirable system of " Housekeeping Centers " now sustained and administered by a committee of men and women on which the settlement has representation.

A flat was rented in a typical Henry Street tenement. Intelligence and taste were exercised in equipping it inexpensively and with furniture that required the least possible labor to keep it free from dirt and vermin. Classes were formed to teach housekeeping in its every detail, using nothing which the people themselves could not procure,—a tiny bathroom, a gas stove, no " model " tubs, but such as the landlord provided for washing. Cleaning, disinfecting, actual purchasing of supplies in the shops of the neighborhood, household accounts, nursing, all the elements of homekeeping, were systematically taught. The first winter that the center was opened the entire membership of a class consisted of girls engaged to be married, —clerks, stenographers, teachers; none were prepared and all were eager to have the homes which they were about to establish better organized and more intelligently conducted than those from which they had come. When one young woman announced her betrothal, she added, "And I am fully prepared because I have been through the Housekeeping Center."

Other centers have been established by the committee in different parts of the city. Dr. Maxwell, Superintendent of Schools, always sympathetic and ready to fit instruction to the pupils' needs, has encouraged the identification of these housekeeping centers with the schools. Whenever an enterprising principal desires it, the teachers of the nearby housekeeping center are made a part of the school system. Perhaps we may some day see one attached to every public school; and I am inclined to believe that, when institutions of higher learning fully realize that education is preparation for life, they too will wonder if the young women graduates of their colleges should not, like our little girl neighbors, be fitted to meet their great home-making responsibilities.

Out of the experience of the originator of the housekeeping centers "Penny Lunches" for the public schools have been inaugurated, and provide a hot noonday meal for children. The committee now controlling this experiment has inquired into food values, physical effects on children, relation to school attendance, and so on.

The schools in a great city have an additional

responsibility, as many of the pupils are deprived of home training because of extreme poverty or the absence of the mother at work, and a measure of failure may be traced to an imperfect realization of the conditions under which pupils live, or to a lack of training on the part of some of the teachers. The Home-and-School Visitor, whose duties are indicated in her title, is charged to bring the two together, that each may help the other; but there are few visitors as yet, and the effect upon the great number of pupils in attendance (over 800,000 in New York) is obviously limited.

We are not always mindful of the fact that children in normal homes get education apart from formal lessons and instruction. Sitting down to a table at definite hours, to eat food properly served, is training, and so is the orderly organization of the home, of which the child so soon becomes a conscious part. There is direction toward control in the provision for privacy, beginning with the sequestered nursery life. The exchange of letters, which begins with most children at a very early age, the conversation of their elders, familiarity with telegrams and telephones, and with the incidents of travel, stimulate their intelligence, resourcefulness, and self-reliance.

Contrast this regulated domestic life with the experience of children—a large number in New York—who may never have been seated around a table in an orderly manner, at a given time, for a family meal. Where the family is large and the rooms small, and those employed return at irregular hours, its members must be fed at different times. It is not uncommon in a neighborhood such as ours to see the mother lean out of the fourth- or fifth-story window and throw down the bread-and-butter luncheon to the little child  waiting on the sidewalk below—sometimes to save him the exertion of climbing the stairs, sometimes because of insufficient time. The children whose mothers work all day and who are locked out during their absence are expected to shift for themselves, and may as often be given too much as too little money to appease their hunger. Having no more discretion in the choice of food than other children of their age, they become an easy prey for the peddlers of unwholesome foods and candies (often with gambling devices attached) who prowl outside the school limits.

Even those students who are better placed economically, or who have the perseverance to go on into the higher schools, may have had no experience but that of a disorganized tenement home. Emil was an instance of this. He  supported himself while attending school by teaching immigrants at night. We invited him to a party at one of our country places and instructed him to call in the morning for his railroad ticket. He failed to appear until long after the appointed hour, not realizing that trains leave on schedule time. Apparently he had never consulted a time-table or taken a journey except with a fresh-air party conducted by someone else. Next morning he returned the ticket, and I learned that he had not reached the farm because he did not know the way to it from the station. Somewhat disconcerted to learn that he had taken fruitlessly a trip of something over an hour's duration, I asked why he had not telephoned to the farm for directions. This seventeen-year-old boy, in his third year in the high school, had not thought of a telephone in the country.   Moreover, he had never used one anywhere.

Happily, there is a growing realization among educators of the necessity of relating the school more closely to the children's future, and it is not an accident that one of the widely known authorities on vocational guidance has had long experience in settlements.[1]

A friend has recently given to me the letters which I wrote regularly to her family during the first two years of my life on the East Side.   I had almost forgotten, until these letters recalled it to me, how often Miss Brewster and I mourned over the boys and girls who were not in school, and over those who had already gone to work without any education. Almost everyone has had knowledge at some time of the chagrin felt by people who cannot read or write.   One intelligent woman of my acquaintance, born in New York State, ingeniously succeeded for many years in keeping the fact of her illiteracy secret from the people with whom she lived on terms of intimacy, buying the newspaper daily and making a pretense of reading it.

[1] "The Vocational Guidance of Youth," by Meyer Bloomfield (Houghton Mifflin Co.).

We had naïvely assumed that elementary education was given to all, and were appalled to find entire families unable to read or write, even though some of the children had been born in America. The letters remind me, too, of the efforts we made to get the children we encountered into school,—day school or night school, public or private,—and how many different people reacted to our appeals. The Department of Health, to facilitate our efforts, supplied us with virus points and authority to vaccinate, since no unvaccinated child could be admitted to school. We gave such publicity as was in our power to the conditions we found, not disdaining to stir emotionally by our " stories " when dry and impersonal statistics failed to impress.

Since those days, New York City has established a school census and has almost perfected a policy whereby all children are brought into school; but throughout the state there are communities where the compulsory education law is disregarded. The Federal Census of 1910 shows in this Empire State, in the counties (Franklin and Clinton) inhabited by the native-born, illiteracy far in excess of that in the counties where the foreign-born congregate.

Wonderful advance has been made within two decades in the conception of municipal responsibility for giving schooling to all children. Now the blind, the deaf, the cripples, and the mentally defective are included among those who have the right to education. When in 1893 I climbed the stairs in a Monroe Street tenement in answer to a call to a sick child, I found Annie F—— lying on a tumbled bed, rigid in the braces which encased her from head to feet. All about her white goods were being manufactured, and five machines were whirring in the room. She had been dismissed from the hospital as incurable, and her mother carried her at intervals to an uptown orthopedic dispensary. A pitiful, emaciated little creature! The sweatshop was transfigured for Annie when we put pretty white curtains at the window upon which she gazed, hung up a bird-cage, and placed a window-box full of growing plants for her to look at during the long days. Then, realizing that she might live many years and would need, even more than other children, the joys that come from books, we found a young woman who was willing to go to her bedside and teach her.

Nowadays children crippled as Annie was may be taken to school daily, under the supervision of a qualified nurse, in a van that calls for them and brings them home. One of these schools, established by intelligent philanthropists, is on Henry Street; the instructors are engaged and paid by the Department of Education. There are also classes in different sections of the city equipped for the special needs of cripples, to give them industrial training which will provide for their future happiness and economic independence.

CHAPTER VI

THE HANDICAPPED CHILD

Educators have only recently realized the existence of large numbers of pupils within the schools who are unequal to the routine classwork because of mental defects. It was one of our settlement residents, a teacher in a Henry Street school, who first startled us into serious consideration of these children. In the year 1899 she brought to us from time to time reports of a colleague, Elizabeth Farrell, whose attention was fixed upon the "poor things" unable to keep up with the grade. She had, our resident declared, "ideas" about them. We sought acquaintance with her, and we felt it a privilege to learn to know the noble enthusiasm of this young woman for those pupils who, to teachers, must always seem the least hopeful.

The Board of Education permitted her to form the first class for ungraded pupils, in School Number 1, in 1900, and the settlement gladly helped develop her theory of separate classes and special instruction for the defectives, not alone for their sakes, but to relieve the normal classes which their presence retarded. We provided equipment not yet on the School Board's requisition list, obtained permission for her to attend children's clinics, secured treatment for the children, and, finally, and not least important, made every effort to interest members of the School Board and the public generally in this class of children.

The plan included the provision of a luncheon. For this we purchased tables, paper napkins, and dishes. The children brought from home bread and butter, and a penny for a glass of milk, and an alert principal made practical the cooking lessons given to the older girls in the school by having them prepare the main dish of the pupils' luncheon —incidentally the first to be provided in the grade schools. Occasionally the approval of the families would be expressed in extra donations, and in the beginning this sometimes took the form of a bottle of beer. Every day one pupil was permitted to invite an adult member of his family to the luncheon, which led naturally to an exchange of visits between members of the family and the teacher.

Among the pupils in this first class was Tony, a Neapolitan, impossible in the grade class because of emotional outbursts called " bad temper," and an incorrigible truant. When defects of vision were corrected the outbursts became less frequent, and manual work disclosed a latent power of application and stimulated a willingness to attend school. Tony is now a bricklayer, a member of the union in good standing, and last spring he and his father bought a house in Brooklyn.

Another was Katie. Spinal meningitis when she was very young had left her with imperfect mental powers. Careful examination disclosed impaired control, particularly of the groups of smaller muscles. She has never learned to read, but has developed skill in clay-modeling, and sews and embroiders very well. She makes her clothes and is a cheerful helper to her mother in the work about the house. Last Christmas she sent to the school warm undergarments which she had made, to be given to the children who needed them. Her intelligent father feels that but

for the discriminating instruction in the ungraded class her powers would have progres-
sively deteriorated and Katie "would be in
darkness."

The teacher who thus first fixed our attention
upon these defective children has long been
a member of the settlement family. She has
carried us with her in her zeal for them, and
we have come to see that it is because the
public conscience has been sluggish that means
and methods have not been more speedily devised toward an intelligent solution of this
serious social problem.

From the small beginnings of the experimental class in Henry Street a separate department in the public schools was created in 1908,
and this year (1915) there are 3,000 children
throughout the city under the care of specially
trained teachers who have liberty to adapt the
school work to the children's peculiar needs.
All these ungraded classes are under the direction of Miss Farrell.

Looking back upon the struggles to win formal recognition of the existence of these children, who now so much engage the attention
of educators and scientists, we realize that our
colleague's devotion to them, her power to excite enthusiasm in us, and her understanding of
the social implications of their existence, came

from a deep-lying principle that every human being, even the least lovely, merits respectful consideration of his rights and his personality.

Much is required of the public school teachers, and many of them rise to every demand; but naturally, in so great a number, there are some who do not recognize that theirs is the responsibility for discovering the children who are not normal. Harry sits on our doorsteps almost every day, ready to run errands, and harmless as yet. Obviously defective, a "pronounced moron," he was promoted from class to class, and when one of his settlement friends called upon the teacher to discuss Harry's special needs, the teacher, somewhat contemptuous of our anxiety, observed that "all that Harry needed was a whipping."

From one-half of one per cent. to two per cent. of children of school age are, it is estimated, in need of special instruction because of the quality or the imperfect functioning of their mental powers. The public school has the power, and should exercise it, to bring within its walls all the children physically and mentally competent to attend it. If children are under intelligent observation, departures from the normal can in many instances be recognized in time for training and education according to the particular need. Long-continued observation and record of the child are essential to intelligent treatment of abnormalities concerning

which there is even now very little accurate information. Cumulative experience and data, such as can be obtained only through the compulsory attendance at school of the multitudes of children of this type, will finally give a basis for scientific and humanitarian action regarding them.

Up to a certain period the child's helplessness demands that every opportunity for development be given him, but that is not the whole of society's responsibility. The time comes when the child's own interests and those of the community demand the wisest, least selfish, and most statesmanlike action. Society must state in definite terms its right to be protected from the hopelessly defective and the moral pervert, wherever found. This constitutes the real problem of the abnormal. At the adolescent period those unfit for parenthood should be guarded—girls and boys—and society should be vested with authority and power to accomplish segregation, the conditions of which should attract and not repel.

Because so much needs to be said upon it, if anything is said at all, I am loath to touch upon the one great obstacle to the effective use of all the intelligence and the resources available for the well-being of these children, the most baffling impediment to their and the community's protection, namely, the supreme authority of parenthood, be it never so inefficient, avaricious, or even immoral.

The breaking up of the family because of poverty, through the death or disappearance of the wage-earner, was, until comparatively recent years, generally accepted as inevitable.

In the first winter of our residence on the East Side we took care of Mr. S——, who was in an advanced stage of phthisis; and we daily admired the wonderful ability of his wife, who kept the home dignified while she sewed on wrappers, nursed her husband, and allowed nothing to interfere with the children's daily attendance at school. When her husband died it seemed the most natural thing in the world to help her to realize her own wishes and to approve her good judgment in desiring to keep the family together. The orphan asylum would doubtless have taken the children from her, leaving her childless as well as widowed, and with no counterbalancing advantage for the children to lighten her double woe. A large-minded lover of children, who gave his money to orphans as well as to orphanages, readily agreed to give the mother a monthly allowance until the eldest son could legally go to work. It was our first " widow's pension."

Our hopes in this particular case have been more than realized. The eldest boy, it is true, has not achieved any notable place in the community; but his sisters are teachers and most desirable elements in the public school system of the city,—living testimony to the worth of the mother's character.

In no instance where we have prevented the disintegration of the family because of poverty have we had reason to regret our decision. Of course, the ability of the mother to maintain a standard in the home and control the children is a necessary qualification in any general recommendation for this treatment of the widow and orphan, and competent supervision is essential to insure the maintenance of these conditions.

At the famous White House Conference on Children, held at the invitation of President Roosevelt, there was practical unanimity on the part of the experts who gathered there that institutional life was undesirable and that wherever possible family life should be maintained. Testimony as to this came from many sources; and keeping the family together, or board-ing the orphan with a normal family when adoption could not be arranged, became the dominant note of the conference.

The children, in this as in many other instances, led us into searching thought many years ago. Forlorn little Joseph had called upon me with a crumpled note which he reluctantly dragged from a pocket. It was from the admitting agent of an orphanage, explaining that Joseph could not be taken into the institution until his head was " cured "; and it gave some details regarding the family, the worthiness of the mother, and her exceeding poverty. The

agent hoped that I might relieve her by ex-
pediting Joseph's admission.

I tried to make the child's daily visit to me
interesting. The treatment was not painful, but
the end of each visit—he came with patient reg-
ularity every day—left me as dolorous as himself. One day I tried, by promise of a present
or of any treat he fancied, to bring out some
expression of youthful spirit—all unavailingly.
"But you must wish for something," I urged;
"I never knew a boy who didn't." For the
first time the silent little lad showed enthusiasm.
"I wish you wouldn't cure my head, so I
needn't go to the orphan asylum."

Unscrupulous parents, I am well aware, often
try to shift the responsibility for their children
upon public institutions, but there are many
who share Joseph's aversion to the institutional
life, and we early recognized that the dislike
is based upon a sound instinct and that a poor
home might have compensating advantages
compared with the well-equipped institution.

There have been great changes in institutional
methods since I first had knowledge of them,
and much ingenuity has been shown in devising
means to encourage the development of individ-
uality and initiative among the orphans. The
cottage plan has been introduced in some institutions to modify the abnormal life of large

congregations of children. But at best the life is artificial, and the children lose inestimably through not having day by day the experiences of normal existence. Valuable knowledge is lost because the child does not learn from experience the connection between the cost of necessities and the labor necessary to earn them. It was somewhat pathetic, at another conference on child-saving, to hear one of the speakers explain that he tried to meet this need by having the examples in arithmetic relate to the cost of food and household expenditures.

The lack of a normal emotional outlet is of consequence, and as a result astute physiognomists often recognize what they term the "institution look." Maggie, an intelligent girl, who has since given abundant evidence of spontaneity and spirit, spent a short time in an excellent orphanage. She told me the other day, and wept as she told it, that she had met no unkindness there, but remembered with horror that when they arose in the morning the "orphans" waited to be told what to do; and that feeling was upon her every hour of the day. In fact, Maggie had stirred me to make arrangements to take her out of the institution because, when I brought her for a visit to the settlement, she stood at the window the entire afternoon, wistfully watching the children play in our back yard, and not joining them because no one had told her that she might.

One is reluctant to speak only of the disadvantages of institutional life, for there are many children rescued from unfortunate family conditions who testify to the good care they received, and who, in after life, look back upon the orphanage as the only home they have known. For some children, doubtless, such care will continue to be necessary, but the conservative and rigid administration can be softened, and the management and their charges delivered out of the rut into which they have fallen, and from the tyranny of rules and customs which have no better warrant than that they have always existed.

Perhaps these illustrations are not too insignificant to record. Happening to pass through a room in an asylum when the dentist was paying his monthly visit, I saw a fine-looking young lad about to have a sound front tooth extracted because he complained of toothache. No provision had been made for anything but the extraction of teeth. An offer to have the boy given proper treatment outside the institution was not accepted, but it needed no more than this to insure better dentistry in his case and in the institution in future. The reports stated that corporal punishment was not administered. When a little homesick lad displayed his hands, swollen from paddling, a request for an investigation, and that I be privileged to hear the inquiry, put a stop, and I am assured a permanent one, to this form of discipline. These are the more obvious disadvantages of institutional life for the child. The more subtle and dangerous are the curbing of initiative and the belittling of personality.

An intelligent observer of the effects of institution life on boys, a Roman Catholic priest, established a temporary home in New York to which they could come on their release from the institution until they found employment and suitable places to board. His insight was shown by his provision for the boys during their brief sojourn with him of a formal table service, and weekly dances to which girls whom he knew were invited. As he astutely observed, the boys often went into common society, or society which made no demands, because, from their lack of experience, they felt ill at ease in a circle where any conventions were observed.

Where life goes by rule there is little spontaneous action or conversation, but the children occasionally give clews to their passion for personal relationships. In an institution which I knew the children were allowed to write once a month to their friends. More than one child without family ties took that opportunity to write letters to an imaginary mother, to send messages of affection to imaginary brothers and sisters, and to ask for personal gifts. They knew, of course, that the letters would never leave the institution.

An unusual instance of intense longing for family life and the desire to " belong " to someone was given by Tillie, who had lived all her life in an orphan asylum. Sometimes she dreamed of her mother, and often asked where she was. When she was ten years old the wife of the superintendent told her that her mother had brought her to the asylum, but that all she could remember about her was that she had red hair. From that day the child's desire to re-establish relations with her mother never flagged. In the files of the asylum a letter was discovered from an overseer of the poor in an upstate town, saying that the woman had wandered there. At Tillie's urgent request he was written to again, and after a search on his part it was learned that she had been declared insane and taken to the hospital at Rochester. The very day that Tillie was released from the orphan asylum she secured money for the trip and went to Rochester. The officials of the hospital received her kindly and took her into the ward where, although she had no memory of having seen her, she identified her mother—doubtless by the color of her hair. The mother, alas, did not recognize her. Two years later the girl revisited the hospital and found her mother enjoying an interval of memory. Tillie told me that she learned "two important things"—that she had had a brother and my name. How I was connected with the fortunes of the family the poor, bewildered woman could not explain, and I have no recollection of her. Tillie followed these clews, as she has every other. She has learned that the brother was sent West with orphans from an Eastern institution, and that he has joined the army. The devoted girl is making every effort to establish a home to which she can bring the mother and brother, utterly regardless of the burden it will place on her young shoulders.

We must turn to the younger countries for testimony as to the wisdom of the non-institutional care of dependent children. In Australia the plan for many years in all the provinces has been to care for them in homes, and in Queensland and New South Wales the laws permit the children to be boarded out to their own mothers. It is encouraging to note the increasing number of responsible people in America who are ready to adopt children. It may not be possible to find a sufficient number of suitable homes to provide for all who are dependent; but once the policy of decentralization is established, other methods will be evolved to avoid large congregations of boys and girls. Two of my colleagues and I have found much happiness in assuming responsibility for eight children. Quite apart from our own pleasure in taking to ourselves these "nieces" and "nephews," we believe that we shall be able to demonstrate convincingly the practicability of establishing small groups of children, without ties of their own, as a family unit. Our children live the year round in our country home, and are identified with the life of the community; and we hope to provide opportunity for the development of their individual tastes and aptitudes.

On the Farm.

Education and the child is a theme of widest social significance. To the age-old appeal that the child's dependence makes upon the affections has been added a conviction of the necessity for a guarded and trained childhood, that better men and women may be developed. It is a modern note in patriotism and civic responsibility, which impels those who are brought in contact with the children of the poor to protect them from premature burdens, to prolong their childhood and the period of growth. Biologists bring suggestive and illuminating analogies, but when one has lived many years in a neighborhood such as ours the children themselves tell the story. We know that physical well-being in later life is largely dependent upon early care, that only the exceptional boys and girls can escape the unwholesome effects of premature labor, and that lack of training is responsible for the enormous proportion of unskilled and unemployable among the workers.

The stronghold of our democracy is the public school. This conviction lies deep in the hearts of those social enthusiasts who would keep the school free from the demoralization of cant and impure politics, and restore it to the people, a shrine for education, a center for public uses.

The young members of the settlement clubs hear this doctrine preached not infrequently. Last June the City Superintendent, addressing a class graduating from the normal school, made an appeal for idealism in their work. He spoke of the possibilities in their profession for far-reaching social service, and named as one who exemplified his theme the principal of a great city school, once one of our settlement boys.

CHAPTER VII

CHILDREN WHO WORK

Bᴇssɪᴇ has had eight "jobs" in six months. Obviously under sixteen, she has had to produce her "working papers" before she could be taken on. The fact that she has met the requirements necessary to obtain the papers, and that her employer has demanded them, is evidence of the advance made in New York State since we first became acquainted with the children of the poor. Bessie has had to prove by birth certificate or other documentary evidence that she is really fourteen, has had to submit to a simple test in English and arithmetic, present proof of at least 130 days' school attendance in the year before leaving, and, after examination by a medical officer, has had to be declared physically fit to enter shop or factory.

No longer could Annie, the cobbler's daughter, by unchallenged perjury obtain the state sanction to her premature employment. Gone are the easy days when Francesca's father, defying school mandates, openly offered his little ones in the labor market. Yet we are far from satisfied. Bessie, though she meets the requirements of the law, goes out wholly unprepared for self-support; she is of no industrial value, and is easily demoralized by the conviction of her unimportance to her "boss," certain that her casual employment and dismissal have hardly been noted, save as she herself has been affected by the pay envelope. Her industrial experience is no surprise to her settlement friends, for she is a type of the boys and girls who, twice a year, swarm out of the school and find their way to the Department of Health to obtain working papers. Bessie's father is a phthisis case; her mother, the chief wage-earner, an example of devotion and industry. The girl has been a fairly good student and dutiful in the home, where for several years she has scrubbed the floors and " looked after " the children in her mother's absence.

Tommy also appeared at the office with his credentials and successfully passed all the tests, until the scale showed him suspiciously weighty for his appearance. Inquiry as to what bulged one of his pockets disclosed the fact that he had a piece of lead there. He had been told that he probably would not weigh enough to pass the doctor. Talking the matter over with Mrs. Sanderson, I learned that the immediate reason for taking Tommy out of school was his need of a pair of shoes. The mother was not insensitive to his pinched appearance. A few days later Tommy was taken to visit our children at the farm, and it was pleasant to see that the natural boy had not been crushed. He devoured the most juvenile story-books and was "crazy" about the sledding. The self-respecting mother was not injured in her pride of independence by a little necessary aid carefully given; and though I have not seen Tommy recently, I am sure that neither he nor his employer lost anything because of the better physical condition in which he entered work after his happy winter at the farm.

This attempt to cheat the law by the very children for whose protection it was designed, and the occasional disregard of the purposes of the enactments by enforcing officials, suggest Alice's perplexity when she encountered the topsy-turvy Wonderland.

It was about twelve years ago that a group of settlement people in New York gathered to consider the advisability of organizing public sentiment against the exploitation of child workers. The New York Child Labor Committee thereupon came into existence, under the chairmanship of the then head of the University Settlement, and that committee has since been steadily engaged in advancing standards of conditions under which children may work. Through legislative enactment and publicity it has endeavored to form public opinion on those socially constructive principles inherent in the conservation of children.

Of necessity child labor laws approach the problem from the negative side of prohibition. To meet the problem positively, the Henry Street Settlement established in 1908 a definite system of "scholarships" for children from fourteen to sixteen, to give training during what have been termed the "two wasted years" to as many as its funds permitted.

A committee of administration receives the applications which come from all parts of the boroughs of Manhattan and the Bronx, and preference is given to those children of widows or disabled fathers whose need seems greatest. Careful inquiry is made by the capable secretary to discover natural inclinations or aptitudes, and these are used as guides in determining the character of the instruction to be given. Three dollars a week—somewhat less than the sum the children might have been earning—is given weekly for two years, during which time they are under continual supervision at home, at school, and through regular visits to the settlement. They are looked after physically, provided with occasional recreation, and, in the summer time, whenever possible, a vacation in the country. The committee keeps in close touch with the educational agencies throughout the city, gathers knowledge of the trades that give opportunity for advancement, and, to aid teachers, settlement workers, parents, and children, publishes from time to time a directory of vocational resources in the city.[1]

Approval of this endowment for future efficiency comes from many sources, but no encouragement has been greater than the fact that, while the plan was still in its experimental stage, my own first boys' club, the members of which had now grown to manhood, celebrated their fifteenth anniversary by contributing three scholarships; and that the Women's Club, whose members feel most painfully the disadvantage of the small wage of the unskilled, have given from their club treasury or by voluntary assessment for this help to the boys and girls.

The children who show talent and those

[1] Because of economic conditions in New York during the winter of 1915 and the compulsory idleness of many unskilled workers, the Scholarship Committee of the Henry Street Settlement, among other efforts for relief, rented a loft in a building near a trade school, and thus made it possible for 160 untrained girls to receive technical instruction, the Board of Education providing teachers and equipment.—THE AUTHOR.

whose immaturity or poverty of intellect makes their early venture into the world more pitiful, have equal claim upon these scholarships.

Pippa was one of the latter. She was scorned at home for obvious slowness of wit and " bad eyes "; her mother deplored the fact that there was nothing for her to do but " getta married." Pippa's club leader's reports were equally discouraging, save for the fact that she had shown some dexterity in the sewing class. At the time when she would have begun her patrol of the streets, looking for signs of " Girls Wanted," the offer of a scholarship prevailed with the mother, and she was given one year's further education in a trade school. After a conference between the teachers and her settlement friends, sample-mounting was decided upon as best suited to Pippa's capacities. She has done well with the training, and is now looked up to as the one wage-earner in the family who is regularly employed.

One of the accompanying charts compares the wage-earning capacity of the boys and girls who have had the advantage of these scholarships with that of an equal number of untrained young people whose careers are known through their industrial placement by perhaps the most careful juvenile employment agency

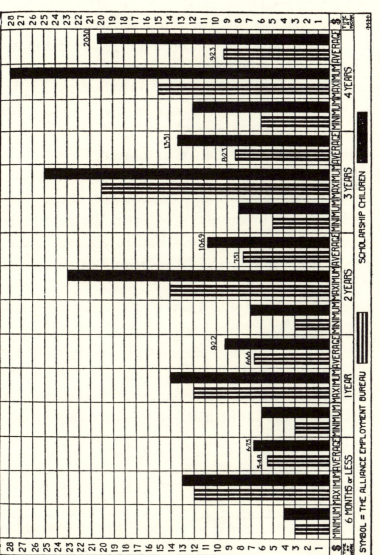

Comparative Weekly Wages of 72 Children Who Have Worked Four Years without Previous Training, from the Record of —— Employment Bureau; and of Scholarship Children Who Have Had Two Years of Vocational Training.

in the city.[1] The deductions that we made from
the experience of the Henry Street children
were corroborated by an inquiry made by one
of our residents into the industrial history of
one thousand children who had applied for
working papers at the Department of Health.
The employment-record chart was compiled
from data obtained in that inquiry.

Our connections in the city enable us occasionally to coax opportunities for those boys
and girls for whom experience in the shop itself
would seem best. Jimmy had lost a leg " hook-
ing on the truck," and his mother supposed that
" such things happen when you have to lock
them out all day." In the whittling class the
lad showed dexterity with the sloyd knife, and
he was thereupon given special privileges in the
carpentry and carving classes of the settlement.
When he reached working age, one of our
friends, a distinguished patron of a high-grade

---

[1] That the ephemeral character of work available for children of
fourteen to sixteen years of age is not peculiar to New York City is
shown by the following figures from the report of the Maryland Bureau of Statistics for the year 1914. In Maryland, working papers
are issued for each separate employment. The number of original
applications in one year was 3,580 and the total of subsequent applications, 4,437. Of the 3,580 children 2,006 came back a second
time, 1,036 a third time, 561 a fourth, 363, a fifth, 194 a sixth,
116 a seventh, 53 an eighth, 29 a ninth, 18 a tenth, and one child
came back for the eighteenth time in a twelvemonth, for working
papers. Many of the children told stories of long periods of idleness between employments.—THE AUTHOR.

decorator, induced the latter to give the boy a chance. Misgivings as to the permanency of his tenure of the place were allayed when Jimmy, aglow with enthusiasm over his work, brought a beautifully carved mahogany box and told of the help the skilled men in the shop were giving him. On the whole, he concluded,

POSITIONS HELD	LENGTH OF TIME IN EACH	KIND OF WORK
FIRST	3 DAYS	IN FACTORY, SORTING BUTTONS
SECOND	2 MONTHS	RIBBONING CORSET COVERS & MACHINE WORK ON THEM
THIRD	I WEEK	RIBBONING & BUTTONING CORSET COVERS
FOURTH	TIME UNKNOWN	LADIES' UNDERWEAR
FIFTH	UP TO CHRISTMAS	ERRAND GIRL
SIXTH	2½ MONTHS	RIBBONING CORSET COVERS
SEVENTH	TIME UNKNOWN	ERRAND GIRL
EIGHTH	A FEW WEEKS	TRIM, CUT, & EXAMINE MENS TIES
NINTH	A FEW WEEKS	RETURN TO SECOND JOB
TENTH	A FEW WEEKS	HOME WORK, RIBBONING

The Typical Employment Record of One Child between the Ages of 14 and 16.

"a fellow with one leg" had advantages over other cabinetmakers; "he could get into so many more tight places and corners than with two."

Bessie and Jimmy and Pippa and Esther and their little comrades stir us to contribute our human documents to the propaganda instituted in behalf of children. In this, as in other experiments at the settlement, we do not believe that what we offer is of great consequence unless the demonstrations we make and the experience we gain are applicable to the problems of the community. On no other single interest do the members of our settlement meet with such unanimity. Years of concern about individual children might in any case have brought this about, but irresistible has been the influence exercised by Mrs. Florence Kelley, now and for many years a member of the settlement family. She has long consecrated her energies to securing protective legislation throughout the country for children compelled to labor and, with the late Edgar Gardner Murphy, of Alabama, suggested the creation of the National Child Labor Committee. In its ten years' existence it has affected legislation in forty-seven states, which have enacted new or improved child labor laws. On this and on the New York State Committee Mrs. Kelley and I have served since their creation.

Though much has been accomplished during this decade, the field is immensely larger than was supposed, and forces inimical to reform, not reckoned with at first, have been encountered. Despite this opposition, however, we believe that the abolition of child labor abuses in America is not very far off.

In Pennsylvania, within a very few years,

insistence upon satisfactory proof of age was strenuously opposed. Officials who should have been working in harmony with the committee persisted in declaring that the parent's affidavit, long before discarded in New York State, was sufficient evidence, despite the fact that coroners' inquests after mine disasters showed child workers of ten and eleven years. The Southern mill children, the little cranberrybog workers, the oyster shuckers, and the boys in glass factories and mines have shown that this disregard of children is not peculiar to any one section of the country, though Southern states have been most tenacious of the exemption of children of " dependent parents " or " orphans " from working-paper requirements.

In the archives at Washington much interesting evidence lies buried in the unpublished portions of reports of the federal investigation into the work of women and children. The need of this investigation was originally urged by settlement people. One mill owner greeted the government inspectors most cordially and, to show his patriotism, ordered the flag to be raised above the works. The raising of the flag, as it afterwards transpired, was a signal to the children employed in the mill to go home. In the early days of child labor reform in New

York the children on Henry Street would sometimes relate vividly their experience of being suddenly whisked out of sight when the approach of the factory inspector was signaled.

It is perhaps unnecessary to mention the obvious fact that the child worker is in competition with the adult and drags down his wages. At the Child Labor Conference held in Washington in January, 1915, a manufacturer in the textile industry cited the wages paid to adults in certain operations in the mills as fourteen cents per hour where there were prohibitive child labor laws and eleven cents an hour where there were none.

The National Child Labor Committee now asks Congress through a federal bill to outlaw interstate traffic in goods produced by the labor of children. Such a law would protect the public-spirited employer who is now obliged to compete in the market with men whose business methods he condemns.

Sammie and his brother sold papers in front of one of the large hotels every night. The more they shivered with cold, the greater the harvest of pennies. No wonder that the white-faced little boy stayed out long after his cold had become serious. He himself asked for ad mission to the hospital, and died there before his absence was noted. After his death relatives appeared, willing to aid according to their small means, and the relief society increased its stipend to his family. At any time during his life this aid might have been forthcoming, had not the public unthinkingly made his sacrifice possible by the purchase of his papers.

Opposition to regulating and limiting the sale of papers by little boys on the streets is hard to overcome. A juvenile literature of more than thirty years ago glorified the newsboy and his improbable financial and social achievements, and interest in him was heightened by a series of pictures by a popular painter, wherein ragged youngsters of an extraordinary cleanliness of face were portrayed as newsboys and bootblacks. In opposition to the charm of this presentation, the practical reformer offers the photographs, taken at midnight, of tiny lads asleep on gratings in front of newspaper offices, waiting for the early editions. He finds in street work the most fruitful source of juvenile delinquency, with newsboys heading the list.

I am aware that at this point numerous readers will recall instances of remarkable achievements by the barefoot boy, the wide-awake young news-seller. We too have known the exceptional lad who has accomplished marvels in the teeth of, sometimes because of, great disadvantages; but after twenty years I, for one, have no illusions as to the outcome for the ordinary child.

When the New York Child Labor Committee secured the enactment of a law making it mandatory for the schoolboy who desired to sell papers to obtain the consent of his parents before receiving the permissive badge from the district school superintendent, we sent a visitor from the settlement to the families of one hundred who had expressed their intention to secure the badge. Of these families over sixty were opposed to the child's selling papers on the street. The boy wanted to " because the other fellows did," and the parents based their objections, in most cases, on precisely those grounds urged by social workers,—namely, that street work led the boys into bad company, irregular hours, gambling, and " waste of shoe leather." Some asserted that they received no money from the children from the sale of the papers. On the other hand, a committee of which I was chairman, which made city-wide inquiry into juvenile street work, found instances of well-to-do parents who sent their little children on the streets to sell papers, sometimes in violation of the law.

The three chief obstacles to progress in protection of the children are the material interests of the employers, many of whom still believe that the child is a necessary instrument of profit; a sentimental, unanalytical feeling of kindness to the poor; and the attitude of officials upon whom the enforcement of the law depends, but who are often tempted by appeals to thwart its humane purpose. A truant officer of my acquaintance took upon himself discretionary power to condone the absence of a little child from school on the ground that the child was employed and the widowed mother poor. Himself a tender father, cherishing his small son, I asked him if that was what he would have me do in case he died and I found his child at work. Oddly enough, he seemed then to realize for the first time that those who were battling for school attendance for the children of the poor and prevention of their premature employment, even though the widow and child might have to receive financial aid, were trying to take, in part, the place of the dead father.

To meet cases where enforcement of the new standards of the law involves undeniable hardship, another form of so-called " scholarship " is given by the New York Child Labor Committee. Upon investigation a sum approximating the possible earnings of the child is furnished until such time as he or she can legally go to work. An indirect but important result of the giving of these scholarships has been the continuous information obtained regarding enforcement of the school attendance law. Inquiry into the history of candidates disclosed, at first, many cases in which, although the family had been in New York for years, some of the children had never attended school, and perhaps never would have done so had they not been discovered at work illegally. The number of these cases is now diminishing.

Allusion to these two forms of " scholarships " should not be made without mention of one other in the settlement, known as the " Alva Scholarship." The interest on the endowment is used to promote the training of gifted individuals and to commemorate a beloved club leader. The money to establish it was given

by the young woman's associates in the settlement, and small sums have been contributed
to it by the girls who were members of her
own and other clubs.

CHAPTER VIII

THE NATION'S CHILDREN

Few people have any idea of the extent of tenement-house manufactures. There are at present over thirteen thousand houses in Greater New York alone licensed for this purpose, and each license may cover from one to forty families. These figures give no complete idea of the work done in tenements. Much of it is carried on in unlicensed houses, and work not yet listed as forbidden is carried home. To supervise this immense field eight inspectors only were assigned in 1913. Changing fashions in dress and the character of certain of the seasonal trades make it very difficult for the Department of Labor to adjust the license list. This explains, to some extent, the lack of knowledge concerning home work on the part of officials, even when the Department of Labor is efficiently administered. Nevertheless, home work has greatly decreased.

Twenty years ago, when we went from house to house caring for the sick, manufacturing was carried on in the tenements on a scale that

does not exist to-day. With no little consternation we saw toys and infants' clothing, and
sometimes food itself, made under conditions
that would not have been tolerated in factories,
even at that time. And the connection of remote communities and individuals with the
East Side of New York was impressed upon
us when we saw a roomful of children's clothing
shipped to the Southern trade from a tenement
where there were sixteen cases of measles.
One of our patients, in an advanced stage of
tuberculosis, until our appearance on the scene,
sat coughing in her bed, making cigarettes and
moistening the paper with her lips. In another
tenement in a nearby street we found children
ill with scarlet fever. The parents worked as
finishers of women's cloaks of good quality, evidently meant to be worn by the well-to-do.
The garments covered the little patients, and
the bed on which they lay was practically used
as a work-table. The possibility of infection is
perhaps the most obvious disadvantage of home
work, and great changes have been wrought
since the days when we first knew the sweatshop; but we are here discussing only its connection with the children.

When work is carried on in the home all the
members of the family can be and are utilized
without regard to age or the restrictions of the

factory laws. One Thanksgiving Day I carried an offering from prosperous children of my acquaintance to a little child on Water Street whose absence from the kindergarten had been

reported on account of illness. He had chicken-pox, and I found him, with flushed face, sitting on a little stool, working on knee pants with other members of the family. They interrupted their industry long enough to drag the concertina from under the bed and to join in singing Italian songs for my entertainment, but the father shrugged his shoulders in dissent from my protest against the continuance of the work.

Examination of the school attendance of children who do home work bears testimony to its relation to truancy. Josephine, eleven years of age, stays out of school to work on finishing; Francesca, aged twelve, to sew buttons on coats; Santa, nine years old, to pick out nut meats; Catherine, eight years old, sews on tags; Tiffy, another eight-year-old, helps her mother finish; Giuseppe, aged ten, is a deft worker on artificial flowers.

It is painful to recall the R—— family, who lived in a basement, all of the children engaged in making paper bags which the mother sold to the small dealers. Something, we know not what, impelled one of the five children to come for help to the nurse in the First Aid Room at the settlement. His head showed evidence of neglect, and when our nurse inquired of him how it had escaped the school medical inspection, the fact was disclosed that he had never been in school. Immediate inquiry on our part revealed the basement sweatshop and the fact that none of the children, all of whom had been born in America, had ever been to school. When the mother was questioned, she answered that she did not like to ask for more aid than she was already receiving from the relief society, and when we reproved the other children in the tenement for not having drawn our attention to their little neighbors, they answered that they themselves had not known of the existence of the R—— children because "they never came out to play." The stupidity of the mother and the circumstances of the family have continually tested the endurance of their well-meaning friends; nevertheless, at this writing the eldest boy is in high school and supporting himself by work outside school hours at a subway news-stand.

What I have written thus far has been in large measure confined to the lower East Side of New York; but it may not be amiss to remind the reader that through the nursing service and other organized work our contact with the tenement home workers extends over the two boroughs of Manhattan and the Bronx. The settlement has never made a scientific study of work done in the homes, but our information regarding it is continuous and current. This cumulative knowledge is probably the more valuable because it is obtained incidentally and naturally, and not as the result of a special investigation, which, however fair and impartial, must be somewhat affected by the consciousness of its purpose.

In 1899 a law was passed in New York State licensing individual workers in the tenements for certain trades. In 1904 this law was superseded, primarily at the instigation of the settlement, by one licensing the entire tenement house, thus making the owner of the house responsible. In 1913 a law recommended by the New York State Factory Investigating Commission was passed by the legislature; this law brought under its jurisdiction all articles manufactured in the tenements, prohibited entirely the home manufacture of food articles, dolls or dolls' clothing, children's or infants' wearing apparel, and forbade the employment of children under fourteen on any articles made in tenements.

All our experience points to the conclusion that it is impossible to control manufacture in the tenements. Restrictive legislation (such as the law forbidding the employment of children under fourteen) is practically impossible of enforcement, for it is a delusion to suppose that any human agency can find out what manufactures are going on in tenement-house homes. The inspectors become known in the various neighborhoods; and at their approach the word is passed along, and garments on which women are working may be hidden, or the work taken from children's hands. The more painstaking and conscientious the attempts at enforcement, the more secretive the workers become, and one is forced to the conclusion that the only practical remedy is to prohibit this parasitic form of industry outright. More of the men in these families would go to work if it were not so easy to employ the women and children; and many of the women would be able to work regular hours in establishments suitably constructed for manufacturing purposes and under state inspection and supervision. During the period of transition, suffering will doubtless come to some families whose poor living has been maintained by this form of industry, and relief measures must carry them over the time of adjustment. Most families working at home are already receiving aid from societies, which thus indirectly help to support the parasitic trade.

In 1913, 41,507 children of Greater New York secured working papers. But the record for 1914 shows a decrease of about 10,000 in the applications for papers, and consequently so many more children in school, because of the amended statute which raised the minimum educational requirement. A public sentiment which keeps boys and girls longer in school emphasizes the need of more educational facilities adapted to industrial pursuits. The children least promising in book studies may often become adepts in manual work, and respond readily to instruction that calls for exercise of the motor energies. The armies of children

who go to work immature, unprepared, uneducated in essentials, with no more than a superficial precocity, are likely to be thrown upon the scrap-heap of the unskilled early in life, and yet many of these have potentialities of skill and efficiency.

It is not surprising that with increasing knowledge of the children's condition plans for their guidance, training, and reasonable employment should have made advance in the last decade. The settlement is now interested in promoting an inquiry for New York City that should lead to the establishment of a juvenile bureau intended to combine vocational guidance and industrial supervision,—a bureau associated with an educational system and dissociated from the free employment exchanges which as yet do not inquire into the character of employment offered.

One outcome of this inquiry has been the formation of a society of employers designed to bring about scientific consideration of the present misemployment of children and adults, underemployment, and other wastes of industry.

We believe that continuation schools are necessary for all boys and girls engaged in shop or factory work, and that expert vocational guidance and educational direction should be offered those who leave school to become wage-earners. It is inevitable that to people at all socially minded close contact with many children should exercise the humanities. The stress that we lay on the enforcement of these protective measures comes from a conviction that the children of the poor, more than all others, need to be prepared for the responsibilities of life that so soon come upon them.

The great majority of the boys and girls

accept passively the conditions of the trade or occupation into which chance and their necessities have forced them. The desire for something different seldom becomes articulate or strong enough to impel them to overcome the almost insuperable barriers. Occasionally, however, the spirit of revolt asserts itself. "I work in a sweatshop," said a young girl who brought her drawings to me for criticism, "and it harasses my body and my soul. Perhaps I could earn enough to live on by doing these, and my brother bids me to display them"; and she added, "I could live on three dollars a week if I were happy." The drawings were promising, and the temperamental young creature, in answer to my questioning, admitted that she had illustrated *David Copperfield* for pastime and had "given David a weak chin."

The difficulty of proper placement in industry experienced by the ordinary boy and girl is intensified in the case of the colored juveniles. It is now nine years since a woman called at the Henry Street house and almost challenged me to face their problem. She was what is termed a "race woman," and desired to work for her own people. It was not difficult to provide an opening for her. The devoted daughter of a man who had felt friendship for the colored people made it possible for us to establish a branch of the settlement on the west side of the city in that section known as San Juan Hill. At "Lincoln House," with the co-operation of representatives of the race and their friends, a programme of social and educational work adapted to the needs of the neighborhood is carried on. To find admirably trained and efficient colored nurses was a comparatively simple matter; and the response of the colored people themselves in this respect was immediately encouraging. Necessity for patient adherence to the principle of giving opportunity to the most needy children, that they may be better equipped for the future, is emphasized in the case of the colored children in school and when seeking work; but difficulties, mountainous in proportion and testing the most buoyant optimism, loom up when social barriers and racial characteristics enter into individual adjustments. The restricted number of occupations open to them discourages ambition and in time reacts unfavorably upon character and ability; and thus we complete the vicious circle of diminishing opportunities and lessening vigor and skill. Colored women are often conspicuously good and tender mothers, and when I have watched large groups of them assembled in their clubrooms, exhibiting their babies with justifiable pride, I have felt a wave

Uses of the Back Yard in One of the Branches of the Henry Street Settlement

of unhappiness because of the consciousness of the enormous handicap with which these little ones must face the future.

A distinguished musician told me not long ago that he gave specially of his time and talent to the colored people of New York because of a debt he owed to a gifted colored neighbor. When he was a boy, his attempts to play the violin attracted the man's attention; the latter offered his services as instructor when he learned that the boy could not afford to take lessons. The colored man had great talent and had studied with the best masters in Europe, but when he returned to America he was unable to obtain engagements or procure pupils, and in order to earn his living was obliged to learn to play the guitar. Discouraging as was his experience, there is, I believe, relatively freer opportunity for the exceptionally gifted of the colored race in the arts and professions than for the ordinary young men and women who seek vocational careers.

Experience in Henry Street, and a conviction that intelligent interest in the welfare of children was becoming universal, gradually focused my mind on the necessity for a Federal Children's Bureau. Every day brought to the settlement, by mail and personal call,—as it must have brought to other people and agencies known to be interested in children,—the most varied inquiries, appeals for help and guidance, reflecting every social aspect of the

question. One well-known judge of a children's court was obliged to employ a clerical staff at his own expense to reply to such inquiries. Those that came to us we answered as best we might out of our own experience or from fragmentary and incomplete data. Even the available information on this important subject was nowhere assembled in complete and practical form. The birth rate, preventable blindness, congenital and preventable disease, infant mortality, physical degeneracy, orphanage, desertion, juvenile delinquency, dangerous occupations and accidents, crimes against children, are questions of enormous national importance concerning some of which reliable information was wholly lacking.

Toward the close of President Roosevelt's administration a colleague and I called upon him to present my plea for the creation of this bureau. On that day the Secretary of Agriculture had gone South to ascertain what danger to the community lurked in the appearance of the boll weevil. This gave point to our argument that nothing that might have happened to the children of the nation could have called forth governmental inquiry.

The Federal Children's Bureau was conceived in the interest of all children; but it was fitting that the National Committee on which I serve, dedicated to working children, should have become sponsor for the necessary propaganda for its creation.

It soon became evident that the suggestion was timely. Sympathy and support came from every part of the country, from Maine to California, and from every section of society. The national sense of humor was aroused by the grim fact that whereas the Federal Government concerned itself with the conservation of material wealth, mines and forests, hogs and lobsters, and had long since established bureaus to supply information concerning them, citizens who desired instruction and guidance for the conservation and protection of the children of the nation had no responsible governmental body to which to appeal.

Though the suggestion was approved by President Roosevelt and widely supported by press and people, it was not until the close of President Taft's administration that the Federal Children's Bureau became a fact, and

the child with all its needs was brought into the sphere of federal care and solicitude. The appointment of Miss Julia Lathrop, a woman of conspicuous personal fitness and adequate training, to be its first chief was a guarantee of the auspicious beginning of its work. In the brief time of its service it has had continuous evidence that the people of these United States intelligently avail themselves of the opportunity for acquiring better understanding of the great responsibility that is placed upon each generation.

The Federal Children's Bureau would not fulfill the purpose of its originators if its service were limited to the study and record of the pathological conditions surrounding children. Its greatest work for the nation should be, and doubtless will be, to create standards for the states and municipalities which may turn to it for expert  advice and guidance. With the living issues involved it is not likely to become mechanical.

The Children's Bureau is a symbol of the most hopeful aspect of America. Founded in love for children and confidence in the future, its existence is enormously significant. The first time I visited Washington after the establishment of the Bureau I felt a thrill of the new and the hopeful, and I contrasted its bare office with the splendid monuments that had been erected and dedicated to the past. Some day, I thought, a lover of his country, understanding that the children of to-day are our future, will build a temple to them in the seat of the Federal Government. This building will be more beautiful than those inspired by the army and navy, by the exploits of science or commemoration of the dead. As my imagination soared I fairly visualized the Children's Bureau developed, expanded, drawing from all corners of the land eager parents and teachers to learn not only the theory of child culture, but to see demonstrations of the best methods in playgrounds, clinics, classes, clubs, buildings, and equipment. The vision became associated with a memory of the first time I saw the Lucca della Robbias on the outer wall of the Florentine asylum and felt the inspiration of linking a great artist with a little waif. But those lovely sculptured babes are swathed. Some day, when the beautiful building of the Federal Children's Bureau is pointed out in Washington, I have it in my heart to believe that the genius who decorates in paint or plastic art will convey the new conception of the child, —free of motion, uplooking, the ward of the nation.

CHAPTER IX

ORGANIZATIONS WITHIN THE SETTLE-MENT

THE settlement, through its preservation of several of the fine old houses of the neighborhood, maintains a curious link with what, in this city of rapid changes, is already a shadowy past. The families of some of the residents once lived nearby, and recall, when they visit us, the schools and churches they attended, their dancing classes, and the homes where they were entertained. One visitor told of the scandal in the best society, more than half a century ago, at the extravagance of a proud father, then an occupant of one of the settlement houses, who gave his young daughter a necklet of pearls on the day of her "coming-out" party. Old men and women for whom the names of the streets evoke reminiscences delight to revive the happy memories of their youth and to identify the few buildings, greatly altered as to their uses, that still remain.

Cherry Street and Cherry Hill, a short distance away, call up traditions of a great orchard to which we owe their names, its beauty in the blossoming time, the quaint, clean houses, each in its garden, all the pleasant, comfortable life of a bygone time. There is nothing pleasant or comfortable about Cherry Street to-day. Legends of the daring deeds of the Cherry Hill gang lend a dubious glamour to some parts of it, but for the rest it is dingy and dull.

We met Lena in one of the dull houses where we had been called because of her illness. The family were attractive Russians of the blond type, and the patient herself was very beautiful, her exceeding pallor giving her an almost ethereal look. The rooms were as bare as the traditional poor man's home of the story-books, but the mother had hidden the degradation of the broken couch with a clean linen sheet, relic of her bridal outfit.

After convalescence Lena was glad to accept employment and resume her share of the family burden. One day she rushed in from the tailor's shop during working hours, and, literally upon her knees, begged for other work. She could no longer endure the obscene language of her employer, which she felt was directed especially to her. The story to experienced ears signaled danger, but to extricate her without destruction of the pride which repelled financial aid was not simple. Readjustments had to be made to

Here and There Are Still Found Reminders of Old New York

give her a belated training that would fit her for employment outside the ranks of the unskilled. Fortunately, the parents needed little stimulus to comprehend the humiliation to their daughter, and they readily agreed to the postponement of help from her, although they were at a low tide of income.

The very coarseness of this kind of attack upon a girl's sensibilities I have learned in the course of years, makes it easier to combat than the subtle and less tangible suggestions that mislead and then betray. Sometimes these are inherent in the work itself.

A girl leading an immoral life was once sent to me for possible help. She called in the evening, and we sat together on the pleasant back porch adjoining my sitting-room. Here the shrill noises of the street came but faintly, and the quiet and privacy helped to create an atmosphere that led easily to confidence.

It was long past midnight when we separated. The picture of the wretched home that she had presented,—its congestion, the slovenly housekeeping, the demanding infant, the ill-prepared food snatched from the stove by the members of the family as they returned from work,—I knew it only too well. The girl herself, refined in speech and pretty, slept in a bed with three others. She had gone to work when she was eleven, and later became a demonstrator in a department store, where the display of expensive finery on the counters and its easy purchase by luxurious women had evidently played a part in her moral deterioration. Her most conscious desire was for silk underwear; at least it was the only one she seemed able to formulate! And this trivial desire, infinitely pathetic in its disclosure, told her story. As I stood at the front door after bidding her good-night, and watched her down the street, it did not seem possible that so frail a creature could summon up the heroism necessary to rise above the demoralization of the home to which she was returning and the kind of work open to her.

During that summer she came each day to the settlement for instruction in English, preliminary to a training in telegraphy, for which she had expressed a preference. Nothing in her conduct during that time could have been criticised, but subsequent chapters in her career have shown that she was unable to overcome the inclinations that were the evil legacy of her mode of life.

The menace to the morals of youth is not confined to the pretty, poor young girl. The lad also is exposed. I could wish there were more sympathy with the very young men who at times are trapped into immorality by means not so very different, except in degree, from those that imperil the girl. The careless way in which boys are intrusted with money by employers has tempted many who are not naturally thievish. I have known dishonesty of this kind on the part of boys who never in after life repeated the offense.

An instance of grave misbehavior of another character was once brought to me by our own young men, three of whom called upon me, evidently in painful embarrassment. After struggling to bring their courage to the speaking point, they told me that L—— was leading an immoral life, and they were sure that if I knew it I would not allow him to dance with the girls. They had been considering for some time whether or not I should be informed. Heartily disliking the task, one of the young men had consulted his mother and she had made it plain that it was my right to know. Fortunately the district attorney then in office had from time to time invoked the co-operation of the settlement in problems that could not be met by a prosecutor. A telephone message to him brought the needed aid with dispatch. When all the facts were known, I felt that the young man had been snared exactly as had been the young girl who was with him. Both were victims of the wretched creature whose exile from New York the district attorney insisted upon. The three had met in a dance-hall, widely advertised and popular among young people.

The inquiry of the famous Committee of Fifteen, as New Yorkers know, was given its first impetus by the action of a group of young men of our neighborhood, already distinguished for the ethical stand they had taken on social matters, and every one of them members for many years of clubs in another settlement and our own. They comprehended the hideous cost of the red-light district and resented its existence in their neighborhood, where not even the children escaped knowledge of its evils.

Although in the twenty-one years of the organized life of the settlement no girl or young woman identified with us has " gone wrong " in the usual understanding of that term, we have been so little conscious of working definitely for this end that my attention was drawn to the fact only when a woman distinguished for her work among girls made the statement that never in the Night Court or institutions for delinquents had she found a girl who had " belonged " to our settlement.[1]

[1] While writing this we learn that a child attending a settlement club has been involved in practices that indicate a perversion, but she cannot properly be included in the above classification because of her extreme youth.—THE AUTHOR.

I record this bit of testimony with some hesitation, as it does not seem right to make it matter for marvel or congratulation. One does not expect a mother to be surprised or gratified that her daughters are virtuous; and it would be a grave injustice to the girls of character and lofty ideals who through the years have been connected with the settlement if we assumed the credit for their fine qualities.

But as in ordinary families there are diversities of character, of strength, and of weakness, so in a large community family, if I may so define the relationship of the settlement membership, these diversities are more strongly marked; and it is a gratification that we are often able to give to young girls—frail, ignorant, unequipped for the struggle into which they are so early plunged—some of the protection that under other circumstances would be provided by their families and social environment.

All classes show occasional instances of girls who " go wrong." The commonly accepted theory that the direct incentive is a mercenary one is not borne out by our experience. The thousands of poor young girls we have known, into whose minds the thought of wrong-doing of this kind has never entered, testify against it.

However, a low family income means a poor

home, underfeeding, congestion, lack of privacy, and lack of proper safeguards against the emotional crises of adolescence for both boys and girls. Exhaustion following excessive or monotonous toil weakens moral and physical resistance; and as a result of the inadequate provision for wholesome, inexpensive recreation, pleasures are secured at great risk.

In the summer of 1912 a notorious gambler was murdered in New York, and the whole country was shocked by the disclosure of the existence of groups of young men organized for crime and designated as "gunmen." There is not space here for a discussion of this tragic result of street life. It is probable that the four young men who were executed for the murder were led astray, in the first place, by their craving for adventure. They were found to have been the tools of a powerful police officer, and it was generally believed that they were mentally defective, and were thus made more readily the dupes of an imposing personality. They had not suffered from extreme poverty, nor had they been without religious instruction. Two of them, in fact, came from homes of orthodox strictness; but it was plain from their histories that there had been no adjustment of environment to meet their needs. There was no evidence that they had at any time come in contact with people or institutions that recognized the social impulses of youth.

At the time of the murder I was in the mountains recovering from an illness. The letters I received, following the disclosure of the existence of the "gunmen," particularly those from young men, carried a peculiar

appeal. Our own club members urged the need of the settlement's extending protection to greater numbers of boys. Some of the young men wrote frankly of perils from which they had barely escaped and of which I had had no knowledge. They all laid stress upon the importance of *preventing* disaster by the provision of wholesome recreation which, as one correspondent wrote, "should have excitement also." Their belief in the efficacy of club control is firmly fixed. A few evenings ago one of the young men of the settlement conversant with conditions, speaking to a new resident, defined a " gang " as " a club gone wrong."

Mothers from time to time come to the Henry Street house for help to rescue their erring sons. They come secretly, fearing to have their sons or the police trace disclosures to them. A poolroom on a nearby street, said to have been,

at one time, a " hang-out " of the gunmen, and its lure evidently enhanced by that fact, was reported to us as " suspicious." The police and a society organized to suppress such places told me that the evidence they could secure was insufficient to warrant hope of conviction. Mothers who suspected that stolen property was taken there, made alert by anxiety for their sons, furnished me with evidence that warranted insistence on my part that the Police Commissioner order the place closed.

Formal meetings with parents to consider matters affecting their children are a fixed part of the settlement programme, and the problems of adolescence are freely and frankly discussed. An experienced and humane judge, addressing one such meeting, spoke simply and directly of the young people who were brought before him charged with crime, showing his understanding of the causes that led to it and his sympathy with the offenders as well as with their harassed parents. He begged for a revival of the old homely virtues and for the strengthening of family ties. A mother in the group rose and confessed her helplessness. She reminded the judge of the difficulty of keeping young people under observation and guarding them from the temptations of street life when the mothers, like herself, went out to work. Ordinary boys and girls, she thought, could not resist these temptations unaided; and speaking of her own boy, who had been brought before him, she summed up her understanding of the situation in the words: " It's not that my son is bad; it's just that he's not a hero."

I do not know who originated the idea of a " club " as a means of guidance and instruction for the young. Our inducement to organize socially came from a group of small boys in the summer of 1895, our first in the Henry Street house. We had already acquired a large circle of juvenile friends, and it soon became evident that definite hours must be set aside for meeting different groups if our time was

not to be dissipated in fragmentary visits. When these boys of eleven and twelve years of age, who had not, up to that time, given any evidence of partiality for our society, called to ask if they could see me some time when I " wasn't busy," I made an appointment with them for the next Saturday evening, whereupon the club was organized.

It is still in existence with practically the original membership; and the relationship of the members of this first group to the settlement and to me personally has been of priceless value. Many of its members have for years been club leaders. They contribute generously to the settlement and in a variety of ways enter into its life and responsibilities.

Clubs formed since then, for all ages and almost all nationalities, have proved to be of great value in affording opportunity for fellowship, and, during the susceptible years, in aiding the formation of character; and the continuity of the relationship has made possible an interchange of knowledge and experience of great advantage to those brought together.

The training of club leaders is as essential as the guidance of the club members. Brilliant personalities are attracted to the settlement, but it can use to good purpose the moderate talents and abilities of more ordinary people whose good-will and interest are otherwise apt to be wasted because they find no expression for them.

Given sincerity, and that vague but essential quality called personality, in the leaders, we do not care very much what the programme of a club may be. I have never known a club leader possessing these qualifications who did not get out of the experience as much as it was possible to give, if not more. An interest in basic social problems develops naturally out of the club relationship. Housing conditions, immigration, unemployment, minimum wage, political control, labor unions, are no longer remote and academic. They are subjects of immediate concern because of their vital importance to the new circle of friends.

The leaders of the clubs meet regularly for inspiration and guidance. Their conferences might be likened to serious faculty meetings,

A Settlement Interior.

only here the social aspects of life and individual problems are discussed. We ask them to bear in mind the necessity of encouraging the altruistic impulses inherent in normal human kind, but, like other faculties, needing to be exercised. Where the material needs challenge the sympathies one must be reminded that "where there is no vision the people

ESTHER

perish." In our neighborhood there are traditions among the people that readily lend themselves to the reaffirmation of this message.

The girls' and children's department has long
had the inspiration of a gifted young woman
who, though a non-resident, has contributed
in equal measure with those who have found it
possible to detach themselves sufficiently from
their family obligations to reside in the settlement. Among the leaders are young men and
women who themselves have been members of
the clubs, some of them now occupying positions of trust and authority in the city.

The classes have more definite educational
programmes, but in the settlement they are in-
terrelated with the clubs and made to harmonize
with their purpose. For children attending
school the manual training is planned to demonstrate the value of new experiments or to
supplement the instruction the school system
affords. The art classes are limited and informal, and without studio equipment as yet, but
interested teachers have given their time to
students who show inclination or ability, and
effort is made to bring out not conventional,
imitative work, but the power to see and to
portray honestly the things about us. All the
settlement family felt that for this reason, if
for no other, it was fitting to have the story

of " The House on Henry Street " illustrated
by one who had found his art expression there.

The dramatic instinct is very strong in the
Jewish child, and musical gifts are not uncommon. With encourage-
ment a high degree of
talent is often developed.
Perhaps the most im-
pressive evidence of this
has been given in the
cycle of Hebrew ritual
festivals, poetical inter-
pretations of the cere-
monies cherished by the
Henry Street neighbor-
hood. The value of
these is not limited to
the educational effect
upon the young people. They interpret anew
to the community the rich inheritance of our
neighbors, and the parents of those who participate give touching evidence of their appreciation.

When a beautiful pageant based on the incident of Miriam and her maidens was in
rehearsal an intractable small boy was dismissed from the cast. In the evening his

father, a printer, called and expressed the hope that if his son's behavior was not unforgivable we would take him back. He wished the boy might carry through life the memory of having had a part in something as beautiful as this festival. After a performance a woman who had suffered bitterly in her Russian home blocked for a moment the outgoing crowd at the door while she stopped to say how beautiful she thought it, adding with deep feeling, " I thank most for showing respect to our religion."

The dramatic club has attempted serious work, and " The Shepherd," by Olive Tilford Dargan, and Galsworthy's " Silver Box " were two of their performances given at Clinton Hall that, in the judgment of the critical, reached a high level of excellence.

The Neighborhood Playhouse, opened in February, 1915, is the outcome of the work of the festival and dramatic groups of the Henry Street Settlement. For nine years gifted leaders have devoted themselvs to this interest, and the building of the well-appointed little theater was necessary for the further development of the work. In addition to the education incident to performing parts in good plays under cultured instructors, and the music, poetry, and dance of the festival classes, the playhouse offers training in the various arts and trades connected with stage production. Practically all the costumes, settings, and properties used in the settlement performances have been made in the classes and workshops.

"Jephthah's Daughter," a festival, opened the playhouse. We were pleased to believe that the performance gained in significance because the music, the dance, and the color were a reminder of the dower brought to New York by the stranger. Seventy-eight young people were in the cast, and many more had a share in the production. Children belonging to the youngest clubs in the settlement pulled the threads to make the fringes; designers and makers of costumes, craftsmen, composers,

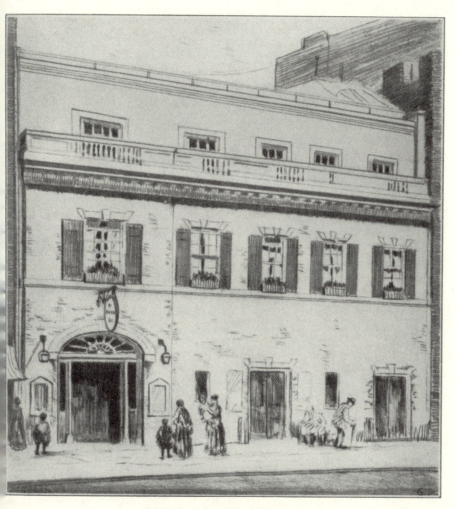

THE NEIGHBORHOOD PLAYHOUSE

painters and musicians, seamstresses, directors, and producers, all contributed in varying degrees, showing a community of interest, service, and enthusiasm only possible when the purpose lies outside the materialist's world.

It is our hope that the playhouse, identified with the neighborhood, may recapture and hold something of the poetry and idealism that be-

From "Jephthah's Daughter."

long to its people and open the door of opportunity for messages in drama and picture and song and story. In its first brief season, beside the productions of the groups for whose development the theater was constructed, there have been special performances for the children at which famous story-tellers have appeared. Important anniversaries have been impressively celebrated. Ellen Terry, of imperishable charm, gave Shakespearean readings on the poet's birthday, and Sarah Cowell Le Moyne gave the readings from Browning on his day. Ibsen and Shaw and Dunsany have been interpreted, and distinguished professionals have found pleasure in acting before audiences at once critical and appreciative.

CHAPTER X

YOUTH

We remind our young people from time to time that conventions established in sophisticated society have usually a sound basis in social experience, and the cultivation of the minor morals of good manners develops consideration for others.

We interpret the "coming-out" party as a glorification of youth. When the members of the young women's clubs reach the age of eighteen, the annual ball of the settlement, its most popular social function, is made the occasion of their formal introduction and promotion to the senior group.  As Head Resident I am their hostess, and in giving the invitations I make much of the fact that they have reached young womanhood, with the added privileges, dignity, and responsibility that it brings.

Intimate and long-sustained association, not only with the individual, but with the entire family, gives opportunities that would never open up if the acquaintance were casual or the settlement formally institutional. The incidents that follow illustrate this, and I could add many more.

Two girls classified as " near tough " seemed beyond the control of their club leader, who entreated help from the more experienced. On a favorable occasion Bessie was invited to the cozy intimacy of my sitting-room. That she and Eveline, her chum, were conscious of their exaggerated raiment was obvious, for she hastened to say, " I guess it's on account of my yellow waist. Eveline and me faded away when we saw you at dancing class the other night." It was easy to follow up her introduction by pointing out that pronounced lack of modesty in dress was one of several signs; that their dancing, their talk, their freedom of manner, all combined to render them conspicuous and to cause their friends anxiety. Bessie listened, observed that she " couldn't throw the waist away, for it cost five dollars," but insisted that she was " good on the inside." An offer to buy the waist and burn it because her dignity was worth more than five dollars was illuminating. " That strikes me as somethin' grand. I wouldn't let you do it, but I'll never wear the waist again." So far as we know, she has kept her word.

Annie began to show a pronounced taste in dress, and gave unmistakable signs of restlessness. She confided her aspirations toward the stage. The young club leader, with insight and understanding, used the settlement influence to secure the coveted interview with a manager. Promptly at the appointed hour on Saturday, when the girl's half-holiday made the engagement possible, Miss B—— went to the factory to meet her. In the stream of girls that poured from it Annie, who had dressed for the occasion, was conspicuous. It required some fortitude on the part of her settlement friend to adhere to their original programme, but they rode on the top of a Fifth Avenue stage, ate ice cream at a fashionable resort, and finally met the theatrical authority, who gave most effectively the discouragement needed.

When Sophie's manner and dress caused comment among her associates. her club leader, who had been waiting for a suitable opportunity, called to see her on Sunday morning, when the girl would be sure to be at home. Sitting on the edge of the bed in the cramped room, they talked the matter over. As for the paint,—many girls thought it wise to use it, for employers did not like to have jaded-looking girls working for them; and as for the finery,—"Lots of uptown swells are wearing earrings."

Contrasted with the girl's generosity to her family the cost of the finery was pathetically small. She had spent on an overcoat for her father the whole of the Christmas gratuity given by her employer for a year of good service, and her pay envelope was handed unopened to her mother every week.

Sophie finally comprehended the reason for her friend's solicitude, and at the end of their talk said she would have done the same for a young sister.

It is often a solace to find eternal youth expressing itself in harmless gayety of attire, which it is possible to construe as evidence of a sense of self-respect and self-importance. It is, at any rate, a more encouraging indication than a sight I remember in the poor quarter of London. I watched the girls at lunch time pour into a famous tea-house from the nearby factories, many of them with buttonless shoes,

In a Club-room

the tops flapping as they walked; skirts separated from untidy blouses, unkempt hair,—a sight that could nowhere be found among working girls in America.

The settlement's sympathy with this aspect of youth may not seem eminently practical, but when Mollie took the accumulated pay for many weeks' overtime, amounting to twenty-five dollars, and " blew it in " on a hat with a marvelous plume, we thought we understood the impulse that might have found more disastrous expression. The hat itself became a white elephant, a source of endless embarrassment, but buying it had been an orgy. This interpretation of Mollie's extravagance, when presented to the mother, who in her vexation had complained to us, influenced her to refrain from nagging and too often reminding the girl of the many uses to which the money might have been put.

At the hearing of the Factory Investigation Commission in New York during the winter of 1914-15 a witness testified regarding the dreary and incessant economies practiced by low-paid working girls. This stimulated discussion, and an editorial in a morning paper queried where the girls were, pointing out that the working girls of New York presented not only an attractive but often a stylish appearance. I asked a young acquaintance, whose appearance justified the newspaper description, to give me her budget. She had lived on five dollars a week. Her board and laundry cost $4. She purchased stockings from push-cart

venders, "seconds" of odd colors but good quality, for ten cents a pair; combinations, "seconds" also, cost 25 cents. She bought boys' blouses, as they were better and cheaper. These cost 25 cents. Hats (peanut straw) cost 10 cents; tooth-paste 10 cents a month. Having very small and narrow feet, she was able to take advantage of special sales, when she could buy a good pair of shoes for 50 cents. Her coat, bought out of season for $7, was being worn for the third winter. Conditions were exceptional in her case, as she boarded with friends who obviously charged her less than she would otherwise have been compelled to pay; but there was practically nothing left for carfares, for pleasure, or for the many demands made upon even the most meager purse; and few people, in any circumstances, would be able to show such excellent discretion in the expenditure of income.

In the tenements family life is disturbed and often threatened with disintegration by the sheer physical conditions of the home. Where there is no privacy there is inevitable loss of the support and strength that come from the interchange of confidences and assurance of understanding. I felt this anew when I called upon Henrietta on the evening of the day her father died. The tie between father and daughter had been close. When I sought to express the sympathy that even the strong and self-reliant need, so crowded were the little rooms that we were forced to sit together on the tenement-house stairs, amid the coming and going of sympathetic and excited neighbors, and all the passing and repassing of the twenty other families that the house sheltered. It would have been impossible for anyone to offer, in the midst of that curious though not ill-meaning crowd, the solace she so sadly needed.

Emotional experiences cannot be made public without danger of blunting or coarsening the fiber of character. Privacy is needed for intimate talks, even between mother and daughter. The casual nature of the employment of the unskilled has also its bearing upon the family relationship. The name or address of the place of employment of the various members of the family is often not known. "How could I know Louisa was in trouble?" said a simple mother of our neighborhood. "She is a good girl to me. I don't know where she works. I don't know her friends."

And the wide span that stretches between the conventions of one generation and another must also be reckoned with. The clash between them, unhappily familiar to many whose experiences never become known outside the family circle, is likely to be intensified when the Americanized wage-earning son or daughter reverses the relationship of child and parent by becoming the protector and the link between

the outside world and the home. The service
of the settlement as interpreter seems in this
narrower sphere almost as useful as its attempts
to bring about understanding between separated
sections of society.

One evening an eloquent speaker addressing
a senior group dwelt upon the hardships of
the older people and
the obligations of
their children to
them. The young
women lingered aft-
er the speaker had
gone, discussing the
lecture and apply-
ing it to themselves.
Though sensitive to
the appeal, they were
loath to relinquish
their right to self-expression. One girl thought
her parents demanded an impossible sacrifice
by insisting on living in a street to which she
was ashamed to bring her associates. The parents refused to leave the quarter where their
countrymen dwelt, and although the daughter
willingly gave her earnings and paid tribute
to her mother's devotion and housekeeping skill,
she said she felt irritated and mortified every
time she returned to her home.

Quite naturally it came about in the beginning of our understanding of the young people that we should take some action to protect them from the disastrous consequences of their ignorance; for it is difficult for the mothers to touch upon certain themes of great import. They are not indifferent, but rather helpless, in the face of the modern city's demands upon motherhood. Rarely do they feel adequate to meet them. Yet they desire that their girls, and the boys too, should be guarded from the dangers that threaten them.

Years ago we invited the school teachers of the neighborhood to a conference on sex problems and offered them speakers and literature. The public has since then become aroused on the subject of sex hygiene, and possibly, in some instances, the pendulum has swung too far; but we are convinced that this obligation to the young cannot be ignored without assuming grave risks. Never have I known an unfavorable reaction when the presentation of this subject has been well considered. It is impossible to give directions as to how it should be done; temperament, development, and environment influence the approach. The girl invariably responds to the glorification of her importance as woman and as future mother, and the theme leads on naturally to the miracle of nature that guards and then creates; and the young men have shown themselves far from indifferent to their future fatherhood. Fathers and mothers should be qualified, and an increasing number are trying to take this duty upon themselves; but where the parents confess their helplessness the duty plainly devolves upon those who have established confidential relations with the members of the family.

At Riverholm.

WHITHER?

(To a Young Girl)

Say whither, whither, pretty one?
The hour is young at present!
How hushed is all the world around!
Ere dawn—the streets hold not a sound.
O whither, whither do you run?
Sleep at this hour is pleasant.
The flowers are dreaming, dewy-wet;
The bird-nests they are silent yet.
Where to, before the rising sun
The world her light is giving?

" To earn a living."

O whither, whither, pretty child,
So late at night a-strolling?
Alone—with darkness round you curled?
All rests!—and sleeping is the world.
Where drives you now the wind so wild?
The midnight bells are tolling!
Day hath not warmed you with her light;
What aid canst hope then from the night?
Night's deaf and blind!—Oh, whither, child,
Light-minded fancies weaving?

" To earn a living."

[*From "Songs of Labor" by Morris
Rosenfeld, translated by Rose Pastor
Stokes and Helena Frank.*]

CHAPTER XI

YOUTH AND TRADES UNIONS

THE portrayal of youth in a neighborhood such as ours cannot be dissociated from labor conditions, and it was not incongruous that some of the deeper implications of this problem should have been brought to us by young women.

In the early nineties nothing in the experience or education of young people not in labor circles prepared them to understand the movement among working people for labor organization. Happily for our democracy and the breadth of our culture, that could not be so sweepingly said to-day. Schools, colleges, leagues for political education, clubs, and associations bring this subject now to the attention of pupils and the public.

Our neighbors in the Jefferson Street tenement where we at first lived had, like ourselves, little time for purely social intercourse. With the large family on the floor below we had established a stairway acquaintance. We had remarked the tidy appearance of a daughter of the house, and wondered how, with her long hours of work, she was able to accomplish it,— for we knew our own struggle to keep up a standard of beauty and order. We often saw her going out in the evening with books under her arm, and surmised that she attended night school. She called one evening, and our pleas-

ure was mingled with consternation to learn that she wished aid in organizing a trades union. Even the term was unknown to me. She spoke without bitterness of the troubles of her shop-mates, and tried to make me see why they thought a union would bring them relief. It was evident that she came to me because of her faith that one who spoke English so easily would know how to organize in the "Ameri-

can " way, and perhaps with a hope that the
union might gain respectability from the alliance. We soon learned that one great obstacle
to the organization of young women in the
trades was a fear on their part that it would
be considered " unladylike," and might even
militate against their marriage.

The next day I managed to find time to visit
the library for academic information on the
subject of trades unions. That evening, in a
basement in a nearby street, I listened to the
broken English of the cigarmaker who was
trying to help the girls; and it was interesting
to find that what he gave them was neither
more nor less than the philosophic argument
of the book I had consulted,—that collective
power might be employed to insure justice for
the individual himself powerless.

The girls had real grievances, for which
they blamed their forewoman. One or two
who tried to reach the owner of the factory
had been dismissed,—at the instance of the
forewoman, they believed. It was determined
to send a committee to present their complaints
and to stand by the girls who were appointed
on it.

The union organized that night did not last
very long, for the stability of the personnel of
the trades union, particularly among women,

cannot always be reckoned on. People as yet step from class to class in America with ease as compared to other countries, and this has obvious democratic advantages; but it is not so fortunate for the trade organizations or for the standardization of the trade itself, which is thus continually recruited from the inexperienced. There is a flux among the workers, the union officials, and the employers themselves. Among women, the more or less ephemeral character of much of their work, their frequent change of occupation, and marriage, all operate against permanency. The girl who knocked at our door that night, to invite us to our first trades union meeting, is now in a profession.

Later, when we moved to Henry Street, Minnie, who lived in the next block, enlisted our sympathy in her efforts to organize the girls in her trade. She based her arguments for shorter hours on their need of time to acquire knowledge of housekeeping and home-making before marriage and motherhood came to them, touching instinctively a fundamental argument against excessive hours for women.

We invited Minnie to a conference of philanthropists on methods for improving the condition of working girls, in order that she might give her conception of what would be advan-

After the Long Day

tageous. Representatives of the various societies reported on their work: vacations provided,
seats in stores, religious instruction, and so on.
"We are the hands of the boss," said Minnie
when her turn came. "What does he care for
us? I say, Let our hands be for him and our
heads for ourselves. We must work for bread
now, but we must think of our future homes.
What time has a working girl to make ready
for this? We never see
a meal prepared. For
all we know, soup grows
on trees."

Minnie, who was head-
lined by the press during
a strike as a Joan of Arc
leading militant hosts to
battle, had no educational preparation for leadership; no equipment beyond her sound good
sense and her woman's subtlety. Speaking once
of the difficulty of earning a living without
training, she told me that her mother could
do nothing but sell potatoes from a push-cart
in the street, "among those rough people."
Then, repenting of her harshness, "Of course,
some of those people must be nice, too, but it
is hard to find a diamond in the mud."

Frequent and prolonged conferences at the
settlement with Minnie and Lottie, her equally

intelligent companion, and with many others, inevitably led to some action on our part; and long anticipating the Women's Trades Union League, we took the initiative in organizing a union at the time of a strike in the cloak trade. The eloquence of the girl leaders, the charm of  our back yard as a meeting-place, and possibly our own conviction that only through organization could wages be raised and shop conditions improved, finally prevailed, and the union was organized. One of our residents and a brilliant young Yiddish-speaking neighbor took upon themselves some of the duties of the walking delegate. When the strike was settled, and agreements for the season were about to be signed by the contractors (or middlemen) and the leader of the men's organization, I was invited into a smoke-filled room in Walhalla Hall long after midnight, to be told that the girls were included in the terms of the contract.

Though its immediate object was accomplished, this union also proved to be an ephemeral organization. For years I held the funds, amounting to sixteen dollars, because the members had scattered and we could never assemble a quorum to dispose of the money.

When, in 1903, I was asked to participate in the formation of the National Women's Trades Union League, I recognized the importance of the movement in enlisting sympathy and support for organizations among working women. To my regret I cannot claim to have rendered services of any value in the development of the League. It was inevitable that its purpose, as epitomized in its motto—" The Eight-hour Day; A Living Wage; To Guard the Home "— should draw to it effective participants and develop strong leaders among working women themselves. Those who are familiar with factory and shop conditions are convinced that through organization and not through the appeal to pity can permanent reforms be assured. It is undoubtedly true that the enforcement of existing laws is in large measure dependent upon watchful trades unions. The women's trades union leagues, national and state, are not only valuable because of support given to the workers, but because they make it possible for women other than wage-earners to identify themselves with working people, and thus give practical expression to their belief that with them and through them the realization of the ideals of democracy can be advanced.

The imagination of New Yorkers has been fired from time to time by young working women who have had no little influence in helping to rouse public interest in labor conditions. My associates and I, in the early years of the settlement, owed much to a mother and daughter of singularly lofty mind and character, both working women, who for a time joined the settlement family. They had been affiliated with labor organizations almost all their lives. The ardor of the daughter continually prodded us to action, and the clear-minded, intellectual mother helped us to a completer realization of the deep-lying causes that had inspired Mazzini and other great leaders, whose works we were re-reading.

More recently a young capmaker has stimulated recognition of the public's responsibility for the well-being of the young worker. Despite her long hours, she found time to organize a union in her trade, not in a spurt of enthusiasm, but as a result of a sober realization that women workers must stand together for themselves and for those who come after them.

The inquiry that followed the disastrous fire in the factory of the Triangle Waist Company in March, 1911, when one hundred and forty-three girls were burned, or leaped from windows to their death, disclosed the fact that the owners of this factory, like many others, kept the doors of the lofts locked. Hundreds of girls, many stories above the streets, were thus cut off from access to stairs or fire-escapes because of the fear of small thefts of material. The girls in this factory had tried, a short time before the fire, to organize a union to protest against bad shop conditions and petty tyrannies.

After the tragedy, at a meeting in the Metropolitan Opera House called together by horrified men and women of the city, this young capmaker stood at the edge of the great opera-house stage and in a voice hardly raised, though it reached every person in that vast audience, arraigned society for regarding human life so cheaply. No one could have been insensitive to her cry for justice, her anguish over the youth so ruthlessly destroyed; and there must have been many in that audience for whom ever after the little, brown-clad figure with the tragic voice symbolized the factory girl in the lofts high above the streets of an indifferent metropolis.

Before the fire the " shirt-waist strike " had brought out a wave of popular sympathy. This was due in part to the youth of a majority of the workers, to a realization of the heroic sacrifices some of them were making (an inkling of which got to the public), and in part also to disapproval of the methods used to break the strike. Fashionable women's clubs held meetings to hear the story from the lips of girl strikers themselves, and women gave voice to their disapproval of judges who sentenced the young strikers to prison, where they were associated—often sharing the same cells—with criminals and prostitutes. Little wonder that women who had never known the bitterness of poverty or oppression found satisfaction in picketing side by side with the working girls who were paying the great cost of the strike. Many, among them settlement residents, readily went bail or paid fines for the girls who were arrested.

Cruel and dramatic exploitation of workers is in the main a thing of the past, but the more subtle injuries of modern industry, due to overstrain, speeding-up, and a minimum of leisure, have only recently attracted attention. It is barely three years (1912) since the New York Factory Law was amended to prohibit the employment of girls over sixteen for more than ten hours in one day or fifty-four hours a week.

The legislation reflected the new compunction of the community concerning these workers, though unlimited hours are still permitted in stores during the Christmas season.

Few people realize what even a ten-hour day means, especially when the worker lives at a distance from the shop or factory and additional hours must be spent in going to and from the place of employment. And in New York travel during the rush hours may mean standing the entire distance.

Working girls, in their own vernacular, have "two jobs." Those who have long hours and poor pay must live at the cheapest rate. Often they are not able to pay for more than part use of a bed, and however generous may be the provision of working girls' hotels, the low-paid workers are not able to avail themselves of these. The girl who receives the least wage must live down to the bone, cook her own meals, wash and iron her own shirt-waists, attend to all the necessary details for her home and person, and this after the long day. The cheapest worker is also likely to be the overtime worker, a fact that is most obvious to the public at Christmas time.

The Factory Investigating Commission, appointed after the Triangle fire to recommend measures for safety, was continued for the purpose of inquiry into the wages of labor throughout the state and also into the advisability of establishing a minimum wage rate. The reports of the commission, the public hearings, and the invaluable contributions to current periodicals are enlightening the community on the social perils due to giving a wage less than the necessary cost of decent living; and as the great majority of employees concerning whom this information has been gathered are young girls, the appeal to the public is bound to bring recommendations for safety in this respect. The dullness of life when pettiest economies must be forever practiced has also been well pictured in the testimony brought out by the commission.

In these chapters I have sought to portray the youth of our neighborhood at its more conscious and responsible period, when the age of greatest incorrigibility (said to be between thirteen and sixteen) has been passed. Labor dis-

cussions and solemn conferences on social problems may seem an incongruous background for
a picture of youth. Happily, its gayety is not
easily suppressed, and comforting reassurance
lies in the fact that recreation has ever for
the young its strong and legitimate appeal;

that art and music carry their message, and
that the public conscience which recognizes the
requirements of youth is reflected in the increasing provision for its pleasures. "Wider use of
school buildings," "recreation directors," "social centers," "municipal dances," are new
terms that have crept into our vocabularies.

Though the Italians have brought charming

festas into our city streets, it was not until I admired the decorations that enhance the picturesque streets of Japan, and enjoyed the sight of the gay dancers on the boulevards of Paris on the day in July when the French celebrate, that it occurred to me that we might bring color and gayety to the streets—even the ugly streets—of New York. For years Henry Street has had its dance on the Fourth of July, and the city and citizens share in the preparation and expense. The asphalt is put in good condition (once, for the very special occasion of the settlement's twentieth birthday, the city officials hastened a contemplated renewal of the asphalt); the street-cleaning department gives an extra late-afternoon cleaning and keeps a white uniformed sweeper on duty during the festivity; the police department loans the stanchions and the park department the rope; the Edison Company illuminates with generosity; from the tenements and the settlement houses hang the flags and the bunting streamers, and the neighbors—all of us together—pay for the band. Asphalt, when swept and cleaned, makes an admirable dancing floor, and to this street dance come all the neighbors and their friends. The children play games to the music in their roped-off section, the young people dance, and all are merry. The first year of the

An Incident in the Historical Pageant on Henry Street, Commemorating the Twentieth Anniversary of the Settlement

experiment the friendly captain of the precinct asked what protection was needed. We had courage and faith to request that no officer should be added to the regular man on the beat, and the good conduct of the five or six thousand who danced or were spectators entirely justified the faith and the courage.

The protective legislation, the new terms in our vocabulary, and the dance on the street are but symbols of the acceptance by the community of its responsibility for protecting and nurturing its precious possession,—the youth of the city.

CHAPTER XII

WEDDINGS AND SOCIAL HALLS

WHEN we came to Henry Street, the appearance of a carriage before the door caused some commotion, and members of the settlement returning to the house would be met by excited little girls who announced, " You's got a wedding by you. There's a carriage there." It was taken for granted in those days that nothing short of a wedding would justify such magnificence.

In one way or another we were continually reminded of the paramount importance of the wedding in the life of the neighborhood. " What! " said a shocked father to whom I expressed my occidental revolt against insistence upon his daughter's marriage to a man who was brought by the professional matchmaker and was a stranger to the girl; " let a girl of seventeen, with no judgment whatsoever, decide on anything so important as a husband? " But as youth asserts itself under the new conditions, the *Schadchen,* or marriage-broker, no longer occupies an important position.

When we first visited families in the tenements, we might have been misled as to the
decline in the family fortunes if we judged

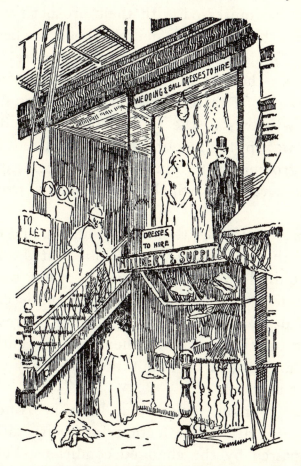

their previous estate by the photographs hung
high on the walls of the poor homes, of bride
and groom, splendidly arrayed for the wedding
ceremony. But we learned that the costumes
had been rented and the photographs taken,

partly that the couple might keep a reminder of the splendor of that brief hour, and also that relations on the other side of the water might be impressed with their prosperity.

Since those days the neighborhood has become more sophisticated, and brides are more likely to make their own wedding gowns, often exhibiting good taste as well as skill; though the shop windows in the foreign quarters still display waxen figures of modishly attired bride and groom, with alluring announcements of the low rates at which the garments may be hired.

We were invited to many weddings, and often pitied the little bride who, having fasted all day as required by orthodox custom, went wearily through the intricate ceremony, reminiscent of tribal days. One bride to whom we offered our congratulations accepted them without enthusiasm, and added, " 'Tain't no such easy thing to get married."

The younger generation, born in America, whose loyalty and affection for their elders is unimpaired by the changed conditions, but for whom the old symbols and customs have no longer a religious meaning, often submit to the orthodox wedding ceremony out of deference to the wishes of the parents and grandparents.

The ceremony in the rented hall (where it

THE OLDER GENERATION

takes place owing to the physical limitations of the home) loses some of its dignity, however much it may have of warmth and affection. To the weddings come all the family, from the aged grandparents to the youngest grandchildren. Before the evening is over the babies are asleep in the arms of their parents or under the care of the old woman in attendance in the cloak-room.

At a typical wedding of twenty years ago the supper was spread in the basement of one of the public halls, and the incongruities were not more painfully obvious to us than to the delicate-minded bride. The rabbi chanted the blessings, and the " poet " sang old Jewish legends, weaving in stories of the families united that evening. We were moved almost to tears by the pathos of these exiles clinging to the poetic traditions of the past amid filthy surroundings; for the tables were encompassed by piles of beer kegs, with their suggestion of drink so foreign to the people gathered there; and men and women who were not guests came and went to the dressing-rooms that opened into the dining-hall. Every time we attended a wedding it shocked us anew that these sober and right-behaving people were obliged to use for their social functions the offensive halls over or behind saloons, because there were no others to be had.

An incident a few days after my coming to the East Side had first brought to my attention the question of meeting-places for the people. As usual in hard times, it was difficult for the unhappy, dissatisfied unemployed to find a place for the discussion of their troubles. Spontaneous gatherings were frequent that summer, and in one of them, described by the papers next morning as a street riot, I accidentally found myself.

It was no more than an attempt of men out of work to get together and talk over their situation. They had no money for the rent of a meeting-place, and having been driven by the police from the street corners, they tried to get into an unoccupied hall on Grand Street. Rough handling by the police stirred them to retaliation, and show of clubs was met by missiles—pieces of smoked fish snatched from a nearby stand kept by an old woman. Violence and ill-feeling might have been averted by the simple expedient of permitting them to meet unmolested. Instinctively I realized this, and felt for my purse, but I had come out with only sufficient carfare to carry me on my rounds, and an unknown, impecunious young woman in

a nurse's cotton dress was not in a position to
speak convincingly on the subject of renting
halls.

Later, when I visited London, I could understand the wisdom of non-interference with the
well-known Hyde Park meetings. It is encouraging to note that common sense is touching
the judgment of New York's officials regarding
the right of the people to meet and speak
freely.

Other occurrences of those early days pointed
to the need of some place of assemblage other
than the unclean rooms connected with saloons.
Walhalla Hall, on Orchard Street, famous long
ago as a meeting-place for labor organizations,
provided them with accommodations not more
appropriate than those I have described. When
from time to time a settlement resident helped
to hide beer kegs with impromptu decorations,
we pledged ourselves that whenever it came into
our power we would provide a meeting-place
for social functions and labor gatherings and a
forum for public debate that would not sacrifice the dignity of those who used it. Our
own settlement rooms were by that time in
constant service for the neighborhood; but it
was plain that even if we could have given them
up entirely to such purposes, a place entirely
free from "auspices" and to be rented—not

given under favor—was required. Prince Kropotkin, then on a visit to America, urged upon
me the wisdom of keeping a people free by
allowing freedom of speech, and of respecting
their assemblages by affording dignified accommodations for them.

It was curious, when one realized it, that

recognition of the normal, wholesome impulse
of young people to congregate should also have
been left to the saloon-keeper, and the young
lads who frequented undesirable places were
often wholly unaware that they themselves
were, to use their own diction, " easy marks."

A genial red-haired lad, a teamster by trade,
referred with pride to his ability as a boxer.
In answer to pointed questions as to where and

how he acquired his skill, he said a saloon-keeper, "an awful good sport," allowed the boys to use his back room. Fortunately the "good sport's" saloon was at some distance; and, suggesting that it must be a bore to go so far after a day's hard work, I offered to provide a room and a professional to coach them on fine points if James thought the "fellows" would care for it. A call next morning at the office of the Children's Aid Society resulted in permission to put to this service an unused part of a nearby building, and during the day a promising boxer was engaged. James had not waited to inquire if I had either the room or trainer ready, and appeared the next evening with a list of young men for the club.

Some weeks later a "throw-away," a small handbill to announce events, came into my hands. It read:

EAT 'EM ALIVE!
Grand Annual Ball of the —— of the
Nurses' Settlement.[1]

The date was given and the price of admission "with wardrobe";[2] and to my horror the

---

[1] We have been popularly known as the Nurses' Settlement, but our corporate name is The Henry Street Settlement.—THE AUTHOR.
[2] Hat and coat checked without charge.

place designated for this function was a notorious hall on the Bowery, its door adjacent
to one opening into " Suicide Hall," so designated because of several self-murders recently
committed there. There was a great deal of
mystery about the object of the ball, and the
instructor, guileless in almost everything but the
art of boxing, reluctantly betrayed the secret.
They had in mind to make a large sum of money
and with it buy me a present. They dreamed
of a writing-desk. It was a difficult situation,
but the young men, their chivalrous instincts
touched, reacted to my little speech and seemed
to comprehend that it would be embarrassing
to the ladies of the settlement to be placed under
the implication of profiting by the sale of liquor,
—though this was delicate ground to tread
upon, since members of the families of several
of the club boys were bartenders or in the
saloon business; but the name of the settlement had been used to advertise the ball, and
" there was something in it."

To emphasize my point and to relieve them
of complications, since they had contracted for
the use of the place, I offered to pay the owner
of the hall a sum of money (one hundred dollars, as I recall it) if he would keep the bar
closed on the night of the dance; and I pledged
the young men that we would all attend and

help to make the ball a success if we could compromise in this manner. The owner of the hall, however, as some of the more worldly-wise members had prophesied, scoffed at my offer.

Public halls are the most common way of making money for a desired end. Sometimes ephemeral organizations are created to " run " them and divide the profits that may accrue. At other times, like the fashionable " Charity " balls, the object is to raise money for a benefi-cent purpose. It required some readjustment of the ordinary association of ideas to purchase without comment the tickets offered at the door of the settlement for a " grand ball," the pro-ceeds of which were to provide a tombstone for a departed friend.

It was soon clear to us that an entirely inno-cent and natural desire for recreation afforded continual opportunity for the overstimulation of the senses and for dangerous exploitation. Later, when the question could be formally brought to the notice of the public, men and women whose minds had been turned to the evils of the dance-halls and the causes of social unrest responded to our appeal, and the Social Halls Association was organized.

Clinton Hall, a handsome, fireproof structure,

was erected on Clinton Street in 1904. It provides meeting-rooms for trades unions, lodges, and benefit societies; an auditorium and ball-room, poolrooms, dining-halls, and kitchens, with provision for the Kosher preparation of meals. In summer there is a roof garden, with a stage for dramatic performances. The building was opened with a charming dance given by the young men of the settlement, followed soon after by a beautiful and impressive performance of the *Ajax* of Sophocles by the Greeks of New York.

The stock was subscribed for by people of means, by the small merchants of the neighborhood, and by settlement residents and their friends. A janitress brought her bank book, showing savings amounting to $200, with which she desired to purchase two shares. She was with difficulty dissuaded from the investment, which I felt she could not afford. When I explained that the people who were subscribing for the stock were prepared not to receive any return from it; that they were risking the money for the sake of those who were obliged to frequent undesirable halls, Mrs. H—— replied, "That's just how Jim and me feel about it. We've been janitors, and we know." The Social Halls Association is a business corporation, and has its own board of directors, of which I have been president from the beginning.

Clinton Hall has afforded an excellent illustration of the psychology of suggestion. The fact that no bar is in evidence, and no white-aproned waiters parade in and out of the ballroom or halls of meetings, has resulted in a minimum consumption of liquor, although, during the first years, drinks could have been purchased by leaving the crowd and the music and sitting at a table in a room one floor below the ballroom. Leaders of rougher crowds than the usual clientèle of Clinton Hall, accustomed to a " rake-off " from the bar at the end of festivities, had to have documentary evidence of the small sales, so incredible did it seem to them that the " crowd " had drunk so little.

It has been a disappointment that the income has not met the reasonable expectations of those interested. This is due partly to some mistakes of construction,—not surprising since there was no precedent to guide us,—largely to the competition of places with different standards which derive profit from a stimulated sale of liquor, and also partly to the inability, not peculiar to our neighbors, to distinguish between a direct and an indirect charge. In all other respects the history of this building has justified our faith that the people are ready to pay for decency. It is patronized by five to six hundred thousand people every year.

CHAPTER XIII

FRIENDS OF RUSSIAN FREEDOM

IF spiritual force implies the power to lift the individual out of the contemplation of his own interests into something great and of ultimate value to the men and women of this and the generations to come, and if, so lifted, sacrifices are freely offered on the altar of the cause, it may truly be said that the Russian Revolution is a spiritual force on the East Side of New York.

People who all through the day are immersed in mundane affairs, the earning of money to provide food and shelter, are transfigured at its appeal. Back of the Russian Jew's ardor for the liberation of a people from the absolutism that provoked terrorism lies also the memory of pogroms and massacres.

Though I had agonized with my neighbors over the tales that crossed the water and the pitiful human drift that came to our shores, I did not know how far I was from realizing the depths of horror until I saw at Ellis Island little children with saber-cuts on their heads and bodies, mutilated and orphaned at the Kishineff massacre. Rescued by compassionate people, they had been sent here to be taken into American homes.

The procession of mourners marching with black-draped flags after the news of the Bialystok massacre, the mass-meetings called to give expression to sorrow at the failure of Father

Gapon's attempt to obtain a hearing for the workingmen on that " Bloody Sunday "[1] when, it will be remembered, the priest led hosts of men, women, and children carrying icons and the Emperor's picture to his palace, only to be fired upon by his order, are some of the events that keep the Russian revolutionary movement a stirring propaganda in our quarter of New York, at least.

Our contact with the members of the Rus-

[1] January 22, 1905.

sian revolutionary committee in New York is close enough to enable us to be of occasional service to them, and some report of our trustworthiness must have penetrated into the prisons, as the letters we receive and the exiles who come to us indicate.

A volume might be written of these visitors. The share they have taken in the revolutionary movement is known, and their coming is often merely an assurance that hope still lives. The young women, intrepid figures, are significant not only of the long-continued struggle for political deliverance, but of the historical progress of womenkind toward intellectual and social freedom.

When Dr. W—— called upon me he was on his way to Sakhalin to join his wife after nearly twenty years' separation. For participation in an act of violence against an official notorious for his brutality and disregard even of Russian justice she had been sentenced to death, but the sentence had been commuted to imprisonment in the Schlüsselburg fortress, whither she was conducted in heavy chains, and where she remained thirteen years. Later she was rearrested and sentenced to exile for life. She had been for five years in the frozen Siberian village of Sakhalin, when, in 1898, her husband, having seen their only son established in life and settled his own affairs, obtained permission from the government to join his wife in her exile.

In imagination I followed this cultured, impressive-looking man on his long journey with a hope that was almost a prayer that the reunited husband and wife would find recompense in their comradeship for all that had been given up and that the woman's fine spirit would make up for whatever she might have lost through deprivation of stimulating contact with her own circle in the world.

My interest caused me to follow their subsequent history. A few years after Dr. W—— had joined his wife they were permitted to remove to Vladivostok. In 1906, after the October manifesto, there was a military revolutionary movement in Vladivostok. The governor gave the order to fire and Madame W——, who, with her husband, was watching the crowd, was killed by a stray bullet. Her son is now a lawyer in Petrograd. Although separated from his mother nearly all his life he shows his devotion to her memory and his sympathy with the cause by defending the "politicals" who come to him.

The settlement from time to time affords occasions for conference on Russian affairs between influential Americans and visiting Russians who entertain hopes of reform by other than active revolutionary methods and it has also given a hearing and found sympathetic friends for other unhappy subjects of the Czar.

Echoes came to us of the persecution of the Doukhobors, a Russian religious communistic sect, whose creed bears resemblance to that of the Friends. Like the active revolutionists, these people had suffered flogging, imprisonment, and exile, but in their case for espousing the doctrine of non-resistance.

In 1897, upon their refusal to take up arms, persecution again became active. The Russian press was forbidden to allude to the subject, but a petition was said to have been thrown into the carriage of the Empress when she was traveling in the Caucasus, where the Doukhobors had been banished, and her interest was aroused. By 1900 Tolstoi had succeeded in fixing attention upon their plight, and arrangements were finally made, chiefly through the efforts of Friends in England and America and the devotion of Aylmer Maude, for their settlement in Canada.

In order to raise funds for the emigration of these peasants to Canada, Tolstoi was persuaded to depart from his established principle and accept copyright for "Resurrection," but the Doukhobors refused to benefit by the sale of a book which they did not consider "good."

During the first years of their life in Manitoba things did not go well with them, and the House on Henry Street became the headquarters for some of their friends as they came and went from England. A young man who, under the influence of Tolstoi, had given up his commission in the army spent a winter in Canada helping them to lay out their farm lands.

When he visited us he paid full tribute to the sincerity of their religious convictions, but somewhat ruefully lamented the fanatical extremes to which they carried them. The Doukhobors, who believed that all work should be shared, voted against one person milking their single cow. "But the cow," said the young ex-captain, "was not a communist, and went dry."

My association with the fortunes of the Doukhobors ended with a slight incident some time later. A peasant, unable to speak any language or dialect that we could command in the house or neighborhood, presented a card at our door on which were written these three words, "Kropotkin, Crosby, Wald." When an interpreter was secured from Ellis Island we

Fraternal greetings P. Kropotkin

learned that, hearing of the pilgrimage of the Doukhobors to Canada, he had decided to follow them, and for clews had only the remote connection of Kropotkin's sympathy with Russian peasants, Ernest Crosby's devotion to Tolstoi, and some rumor of his and my interest in these people. That he should have succeeded in finding me seemed quite remarkable. He was sent to Canada, and subsequent letters from him gave evidence of his contentment with the odd sect to which he had been attracted.

After rather serious conflict between their religious practices and the Canadian regulations, the Doukhobors are reported to have settled their differences and to have established flourishing communistic colonies where thousands of acres have been brought under cultivation.

The Friends of Russian Freedom, a national association with headquarters in New York, is composed of well-known American sympathizers, and, like the society of the same name in England, recognizes the spirit that animates Russians engaged in the struggle for political freedom, and is watchful to show sympathy and give aid.

An occasion for this arose about eight years ago, when the Russian Government demanded the extradition of one Jan Pouren as a common criminal. The Commissioner before whom the case was brought acceded to Russia's demands and Pouren was held in the Tombs prison to await extradition. Then this insignificant Lettish peasant became a center of protest. Pouren, it was known, had been involved in the Baltic uprisings, and acquiescence in Russia's demands for his extradition would imperil thousands who, like him, had sought a refuge here, and would take heart out of the people who still clung to the party of protest throughout Russia. A great mass-meeting held in Cooper Union bore testimony to the tenacity with which high-minded Americans clung to the cherished traditions of their country. Able counsel generously offered their services, and it was hoped that this and other expressions of public protest would induce the Secretary of State to order the case reopened.

My own participation came about because of a request from the members of the Russian Revolutionary Committee in New York that I present to President Roosevelt personally the arguments for the reopening of the case. An hour preceding the weekly Cabinet meeting was appointed for my visit. I took to the White House an extraordinary letter sent by Lettish peasants, now hard-working and law-abiding, residents of Massachusetts and New Hampshire. It read: "We hear Jan Pouren is in prison, that he is called a criminal. We called him 'brother' and 'comrade.' Do not let him fall into the hands of the bloodthirsty vampire." To this letter were appended the signatures and addresses of men who had been in the struggle in Russia and who, by identifying themselves with Pouren, placed themselves in equal jeopardy should the case go against him. They offered to give sworn affidavits, or to come in person to testify for the accused. With the letter had come a considerable sum of money which the signers had collected from their scanty wages for Pouren's defense. I also had with me a translation of the report to the second Duma on the Baltic uprisings wherein this testimony, in reference to the attempt of the Government to locate those involved in the disturbances, was recorded: "They beat the eight-year-old Anna Pouren, demanding of her that she should tell the whereabouts of her father."

The President and the Secretaries concerned discussed the matter, and I left with the assurance that the new evidence offered would justify the reopening of the case. At the second hearing the Commissioner's decision was reversed and Russia's demands refused, on the ground that the alleged offenses were shown to be political and "not in any one instance for personal grievance or for personal gain." [1]

George Kennan, who first focused the attention of Americans upon the political exiles through his dramatic portrayal of their condition in the Siberian prisons, is still the eager champion of their cause. Prince Kropotkin, who thrilled the readers of the *Atlantic Monthly* with his "Autobiography of a Revolutionist"; [2] Tschaikowsky, Gershuni, Marie Sukloff [3]—a long procession of saints and martyrs, sympathizers, and supporters—have crossed the threshold of the House on Henry Street and stirred deep feeling there. Katharine Breshkovsky (Babuschka, little grandmother) [4], most beloved of all who have suffered for the great cause, is to many a symbol of the Russian revolution.

Who of those that sat around the fire with her in the sitting-room of the Henry Street house can ever forget the experience? We knew vaguely the story of the young noblewoman's

[1] U. S. Commissioner S. M. Hitchcock's decision, delivered March 30, 1909.

[2] Now published, with considerable additions, as "Memoirs of a Revolutionist" (Houghton Mifflin Co.).

[3] See "The Life Story of a Russian Exile," by Marie Sukloff (The Century Co.).

[4] See the sympathetic sketch, "Katharine Breshkovsky," by Ernest Poole (Charles H. Kerr & Co., Chicago).

attempt to teach the newly freed serfs on her father's estate in the early sixties; how her religious zeal to give all that she had to the poor was regarded as dangerous by the Czar's government, and how one suppression and persecution after another finally drove her into the circle of active revolutionists. Her long incarceration in the Russian prison and final sentence to the Kara mines and hard labor was known to us, and we identified her as the woman whose exalted spirit had stirred Mr. Kennan when he met her in the little Buriat hamlet on the frontier of China so many years ago.

And then, after two decades of prison and Siberian exile, she sat with us and thrilled us with glimpses of the courage of those who answered the call. Lightly touching on her own share in the tragic drama, she carried us with her on the long road to Siberia among the politicals and the convicts who were their companions, through the perils of an almost successful escape with three students to the Pacific, a thousand miles away. She told of her recapture and return to hard labor in the Kara mines; of the unspeakable outrages, and the heroic measures her companions there took to draw attention to the prisoners' plight, and how, despite these things, she looked back upon that time as wonderful because of the beautiful and valiant souls who were her fellow-prisoners and companions, young women who had given up more than life itself for the great cause of liberty.

Her visit to America in 1905 was made at a time when the long-cherished hopes of the revolutionists had some promise of realization. It was deemed necessary to gain the utmost sympathy and support from the comrades here, and she did indeed reawaken in the hearts of our neighbors their most passionate desire for the political emancipation of a country so well beloved from a government so well hated.

I accompanied Madame Breshkovsky to a reception given in her honor by her fellow-countrymen, and her approach was the signal for a great demonstration. They lifted her from the floor and carried her, high above the heads of the people, to her chair. They sang " The Marseillaise," and the men wept with the women. Love and deference equally were accorded to her noble character and fine perceptions. In addition to her clear and far-sighted vision, her gift of quick and accurate decision and her extraordinary ability as an organizer gave her, I was told, remarkable authority in the councils of her party.

When I last saw her, at the close of her stay in this country, she implored me never to forget

Russia and the struggle there, and said, as we separated after a lingering embrace: "Should you ever grow cold, bring before your mind the procession of men and women who for years have gone in the early dawn of their lives to execution, and gladly, that others might be free."

Upon returning to Russia she was arrested, and after almost three years' imprisonment in the Fortress of Peter and Paul, "that huge stone coffin," was sent to Siberia "*na poselenie,*" as a forced colonist. The first letters that came to her friends from Siberia told of the journey to the place of her exile in the Trans-Baikal, two or three hundred miles northeast of Irkutsk. They traveled by train, on foot, in primitive carts, or "crowded like herrings in a barrel" in boats that floated with the current, having no other means of propulsion, and, finally, after nearly three months spent on the way, reached the little island town of Kirensk, surrounded by two rivers, "the immense and cold Lena and the less majestic Kyrenga."

A letter from a fellow-exile, written in August, 1910, tells of her passing through his village in a company of two hundred and fifty political exiles and criminals, surrounded by a numerous guard. "Among the crowd in gray coats, under gray skies and rain, her imposing figure struck everyone." He notes how her first thought, after days of travel through the pouring rain in a miserable cart, and nights spent in barracks or around a bonfire in the open air, was for others, " our unfortunate comrades." " Their sufferings," he adds, " do a terrible sore at her heart. . . . She formed the center of the party and the object of general attention, not only of her political comrades, but also of the criminals and the soldiers of the convoy. When I had traveled under escort to our exile some months before everywhere we heard ' Babuschka is coming. God grant us to see her!' The prisoners and the exiles in Siberia waited with reverence to see the miracle woman. She kissed us all and cheered us all."

Her attempted escape from Kirensk, recapture, and sentence to the Irkutsk prison in the winter of 1913 are known to all the world. Her letters to American friends from her Siberian exile revealed the heroic soul. Her physical sufferings were only incidentally alluded to, as in one letter where, in the quaint English acquired in America and by study during her last imprisonment, she said: " My gait is not yet sure enough, and it will take some time before my forces and my celerity rejoin me to the point as to let me exercise my feet without the aid of anyone." Nevertheless, she continues

"Babuschka, Little Grandmother"

quite undaunted, "I hope to restore my health and to live till the day I see you again."

The sufferings and deprivations of the young political exiles caused her the greatest sorrow. It was, indeed, the only suffering she acknowledged, although she deplored that reasonable conversation was impossible, with the spies always within sight and hearing, and expressed her "disgust" that they accompanied her whenever she went out.

In Kirensk there are over a thousand exiles forced to live on their earnings and the small stipend received from the government. There is little work to be had, and that little is rendered more uncertain by the fact that the police shift the exiles about, seldom allowing them to remain in one place for more than six months. Most of them are thus kept in a state of semi-starvation. The magazines, books, and picture post cards which Madame Breshkovsky received were used by her to extraordinary advantage. Of some periodicals that I had caused to be sent her she wrote: "They make a great parade in Siberia, going as far as Irkutsk and Yakutsk, and some of them find resting-place in the libraries and museums." She taught English to the young "politicals" and reading and writing to the illiterate native Siberians. "You understand my situation," she wrote: "an old

mother who would serve every one of them. I
aid, I grumble, I sustain, I hear confessions
like a priest, I give counsel and admonition,
but this is a drop in the ocean of misery." And
of herself again: " How happy I am; persecuted, banished, and yet beloved."

From the letters that have come to America
and are shared by the circle of her friends here
I select one, written in answer to a request that
she send a message of her philosophy to the
students of a women's college who had asked
me to tell the story of the Russian revolution as
personified in her:

" October 20, 1913, Kirensk.

" Very dear and well-beloved Lillian:—

" Your letter, as well as the postal cards which
you were good enough to send me, were received by me several days ago, and perhaps it
is with the last mail that I send you this reply.
Snow already covers the mountainous borders
of the superb Lena, and frost will soon fill the
waters with masses of ice, which will interrupt
all communications for two or three weeks,
leaving us isolated on our little island, entirely
engulfed by cold, badly treated by the north
wind. I hasten, therefore, to thank you for
your indefatigable attention towards the old
recluse who, habituated as she is to pass her

days now and again imprisoned or exiled, re-
joices, nevertheless, to find herself loved—to
feel that the most noble hearts beat in unison
with hers.

"It is strange! Every time that I am asked
to speak about myself I am always confused
and find nothing to say. It is very likely that
if I paid more attention to the exterior circumstances of my life there would be enough to
talk about that would fill more than a book.
But ever since my childhood I have had the
habit of creating a spiritual life, an interior
world, which responded better to my spiritual
taste. This imaginary world has had the upper
hand over the real world in its details, over all
that is transient.

"The aim of our existence, the perfecting of
human nature, was always present to my vision,
in my mind. The route, the direction that we
ought to take in order to approach our ideal,
was for me a problem, the solution of which
absorbed the efforts of my entire life. I was
implacable for myself, for my weaknesses, knowing that to serve a divine cause we must sincerely love the object of our devotion, that is
to say, in this case, humanity.

"These meditations, and a vigorous imagination, which always carried me far beyond the
present, permitting me to inhabit the most

longed-for regions, combined to attract very little of my attention to daily circumstances.

"Without doubt, I have had suffering in my life, as I have had moments of joy, of happiness even. It is also true that the struggle with my failings, with the habits engrafted by a worldly education, have cost me more or less dearly. The misery of those near to me tore my heart to the extreme. In a word, life has passed in the same way as a bark thrown upon the mercy of a sea often stormy. But as the ideal was always there, present in my heart and in my mind, it guided me in my course, it absorbed me to such a degree that I did not feel in all their integrity the influences of passing events. *The duty to serve the divine cause of humanity in its entirety, that of my people in particular, was the law of my life,*—the supreme law, whose voice stilled my passions, my desires, in short, my weaknesses. . . .

"Since I live in my thoughts more than by emotion, it is my thoughts that I have to confess more than the facts of my life. These facts, to tell the truth, are sufficiently confused in my memory, and often I would not be able to relate them in all their details. Also, in conversing with those who care to listen to me, I feel that I am monotonous, for it is always my ideas and my abstract observations that I want to communicate to my listeners. I have studied a great deal in order to understand even ever so little of the origin of the human soul, in order to understand more or less its complexity of to-day. There lies my only strength, so to speak, and I continue my study, knowing how complex my object of study is, and what an innumerable quantity of different combinations, of types, of low types, have been formed during the long history of the laboratory where is prepared the supreme fusion called the human soul.

" The esteem for the individual of the human species, and the adoration of the intellectual treasure of this individual, ought to form the center of all religion, of all knowledge, of all ideal. *It is only in venerating the human being as the most beautiful creation of the world, it is only in understanding the beauty and the indestructible grandeur of an intelligence illuminated by love and knowledge, that the education of the young generations will bring the desired fruits. . . .*

" Lillian, my friend, I hope to be understood by you. . . I embrace you. I kiss your two hands and thank you for your noble and dear existence. To your entire settlement I send greetings.

" Your

" Katharine Breshkovsky."

Madame Breshkovsky's friends are to be found in every civilized nation, and her influence, from an exile's hut in an isolated village in the Arctic Circle, has radiated to remote quarters of the globe. From her prison at Irkutsk this woman, nearing her seventieth birthday, sends messages of hope and cheer, proclaiming her unquenchable faith that the cause is just, and therefore must prevail.

I would not have our profound interest in the Russian revolution entirely explained by the fellowship we have had with those who have participated in it, by the literature which has stirred hearts and minds everywhere, or by our actual experience with innocent victims of outrages. The continuance of a policy of suppression of freedom infiltrates the social order everywhere, destroys the germination of new forms of social life, and he who has not sympathy with the throbbing of the human heart, and who does not revolt against injustice anywhere in the world, who does not see in the gigantic struggle in Russia a world movement for freedom and progress that is our struggle too, will not comprehend the significance of the sympathy of the many Americans who are friends of Russian freedom.

CHAPTER XIV

SOCIAL FORCES

It would be impossible to give adequate presentation of those forces termed social which have hold upon our neighborhood.

People with an ephemeral interest in the social order and some who are only seeking new thrills are prone to look upon the East Side as presenting a picturesque and alluring field for experimentation, and they are, at times, responsible for the confused conception of the neighborhood in the public mind.

The poor and the unemployed, the sick, the helpless, and the bewildered, unable to articulate their woes, are with us in great numbers. These, however, comprise only a part of our diverse, cosmopolitan population. There are many men and women living on the East Side who give keen scrutiny to measures for social amelioration. They are likely to appreciate the sincerity of messages whether these relate to living conditions, to the drama, or to music. Not only the East Side " intellectuals," but the alert proletariat, may furnish propagandists of important social reforms.

The contrast between the character of the religious influences of the remoter past, or even of twenty or thirty years ago, in our part of the city, with those of the present day, is marked in the church edifices themselves.

Across from the settlement's main houses on Henry Street stands All Saints', with its slave gallery, calling up a picture of the rich and fashionable congregation of long ago. For years after their removal to other parts of the city, sentiment for the place, focusing on the stately, young-minded, octogenarian clergyman who remained behind, occasionally brought old members back, but now he too is gone, and the services echo to empty pews. The Floating Church, moored to its dock nearby, was removed but yesterday. Mariners' Temple and the Church of the Sea and Land still stand, and suggest an invitation to the seafaring man to worship in Henry Street.

Occasionally a zealot seeks to rekindle in the churches of our neighborhood the fire that once brightened their altars, and social workers hailed one as " comrade " who ventured to bring the infamy of the red-light district to the knowledge of his bishop and the city. That bishop, humane and socially minded, came down for a short time to live among us, and in the evenings when he crossed the crowded street to call or

to dine with us he dwelt upon the pleasure he
had in learning to know the self-respect and

" All Saints'," on Henry Street.

dignity of his East Side parishioners. He spoke
with gratification of the fact that during his
stay downtown no begging letters had come to

him from the neighborhood, nor had anyone belonging to it taken advantage of his presence to ask for personal favors. The neighborhood took his presence quite simply, regretting, with him, the spectacular featuring of his visit by the newspapers. Indeed, the only cynical comment that came to my ears was from a young radical, who, hearing of the bishop's tribute, said: "That's nothing new. It's only new to a bishop."

In the Roman Catholic churches the change is most marked by the dwindling of the large Irish congregations and the coming of the Italians. Patron saints' days are celebrated with pomp and elaborate decoration. Arches of light festoon the streets, altars are erected on the sidewalk, and the image of the saint is enshrined on the church facade high above the passer-by. Threading in and out of the throngs are picturesquely shawled women with lovely babes in arms, fakirs and beggars, venders offering for sale rosaries, candles, and holy pictures. Mulberry, Elizabeth and even Goerck Streets' sordid ugliness is then transformed for the time, and a clew is given to the old-world influence of the Church through drama.

The change from the Russian pale where the rabbi's control is both civil and spiritual to a

new world of complex religious and political authority, or lack of authority, accentuates the
difficulties of readjustment for the pious Jew.
The Talmudic students, cherished in the old
country and held aloof from all questions of
economic needs because of their learning and
piety, find themselves without anchor in the
new environment and precipitated into entirely
new valuations of worth and strength.

Freedom and opportunity for the young
make costly demands upon the bewildered elders,
who cling tenaciously to their ancient religious
observances. The synagogues are everywhere—
imposing or shabby-looking buildings—and the
chevras, sometimes occupying only a small room
where the prescribed number meet for daily
prayer. Often through the windows of a dilapi-
dated house the swaying figures of the devout
may be seen with prayer-shawl and phylactery
and eyes turned to the East. At high festivals
every pew and bench are occupied and additional
halls are rented where services are held for those
men, women, and young people who, indifferent
at other times, then meet and pray together.

But though the religious life is abundantly in
evidence through the synagogues and the *Tal-
mud-Torah* schools[1] and the *Chedorim,* where

[1] Report of the Federal Bureau of Education for 1913 shows
500 of these schools in New York City.

the boys, confined for many hours, study Hebrew and receive religious instruction, and although the *Barmitzvah,* or confirmation of the son at thirteen, is still an impressive ceremony and the occasion of family rejoicing, there is lament on the part of the pious that the house of worship and the ritualistic ceremonial of the Jewish faith have lost their hold upon the spiritual life of the younger generation.

For them new appeals take the place of the old religious commands. The modern public-spirited rabbi offers his pulpit for the presentation of current social problems. Zionism with its appeal for a spiritual nationalism, socialism with its call to economic salvation, the extension of democracy through the enfranchisement of women, the plea for service to humanity through social work, stir the younger generation and give expression to a religious spirit.

Settlements suffer at times from the criticism of those who sincerely believe that, without definite religious propaganda, their full measure of usefulness cannot be attained. It has seemed to us that something fundamental in the structure of the settlement itself would be lost were our policy altered. All creeds have a common basis for fellowship, and their adherents may work together for humanity with mutual respect

THE SYNAGOGUES ARE EVERYWHERE—IMPOSING OR SHABBY-LOOKING
BUILDINGS

and esteem for the conviction of each when these are not brought into controversy. Protestants, Catholics, Jews, an occasional Buddhist, and those who can claim no creed have lived and served together in the Henry Street house contented and happy, with no attempt to impose their theological convictions upon one another or upon the members of the clubs and classes who come in confidence to us.

During any election campaign the swarming, gesticulating, serious-looking street crowds of our neighborhood are multiplied and intensified. Orators, not a few small boys among them, appear on nearly every street corner, and an observer might almost measure the forces that influence the people by the number and character of the orators, the appeals upon which they base their hope of approval at the polls, and the reaction of the crowds that surround them.

Pleas supported by reasonable show of argument are likely to find intelligent response, although, as is but natural, the judgment of a temperamental people is at times not clearly defined. During the recent almost riotous support of a Governor who had been impeached (it was generally believed at the behest of an irritated "boss" to whom he had refused obedience) many New Yorkers who had come to count upon the East Side for insight and understanding were perplexed at what seemed heroworship of a man against whom charges of misappropriation of funds had been sustained. Those who knew the people discerned an emotional desire for justice mingled with some grati-

tude to the man who, while in Congress, had kept faith with his constituents on matters vital to them. Stopping at a sidewalk stand on Second Avenue, I asked the owner what it was all about. "Oh," said he, "Sulzer ain't being punished now for bein' bad. Murphy's hittin' him for the good he done."

Our first realization of the dominating influence of political control upon the individual and collective life of the neighborhood came, naturally enough, through the gossip of our new acquaintances when we came to live downtown, and we were not long oblivious to the power invested in quite ordinary men whom we met.

Two distinguished English visitors to America, keen students and historians of social movements, expressed a desire to learn of the methods of Tammany Hall from someone in its inner councils. A luncheon with a well-known and continuous officeholder was arranged by a mutual friend. When my interest was first aroused in the political life of the city this man's position in the party had been cited as an example of the astuteness of the " Boss." He had revolted against certain conditions and had shown remarkable ability in building up an opposition within the party. Ever after he had enjoyed unchallenged some high-salaried office.

Under the genial influence of our host, and perhaps because he felt secure with the English guests, the " Judge " (he had at one time presided in an inferior court) talked freely of the details about which they were curious,—how the organization tested the loyalty of its members and increased their power and prestige as their record warranted it, giving, incidentally, an interesting glimpse of the human elements in the great political machine. His own success as judge he attributed to the fact that he had used common sense where his highly educated colleagues would have used text-books, and with keen appreciation of the humor of the situation he told how, when he was sworn in, a distinguished jurist said he had come to his court " to see Judge ——— dispense with justice." He defended the logic, from the "Boss's" point of view, of efficiently administering such patronage as was available, and made much of the kindness to the poor that was possible because of the district control. Comparing their own with what he supposed to be my attitude to the poor, he added with a smile of comprehension, "It's the same thing, only *we* keep books."

A political organization watchful to capture personal loyalty makes dramatic appeal, the potency of which cannot be ignored. The speedy release of young offenders from jail was, years ago, the most impressive demonstration of beneficent influence, and it was whispered that district leaders were notified by the police of arrests, that they might have an opportunity to get the young men out of trouble. Certain it is that several times when anxious relatives rushed to us for help we found that the leader had been as promptly notified as the families themselves.

So much genuine kindness is entwined with the administration of this district control that one can well comprehend the loyalty that it wins; and it is not the poor, jobless man who, at election times, remembers favors of whom we are critical.

Opposed to the solidarity of the long dominant party are the other party organizations and numerous cliques of radicals, independents, and reformers. These, when the offenses of the party in power become most flagrant, unite, and New York is temporarily freed from "boss" rule, to enjoy a respite of "reform administration." Into such "moral campaigns" the House on Henry Street has always entered, and sometimes it has helped to initiate them, though steadily refusing to be brought officially into a political party or faction. Indeed, it would be impossible to range residents or club members under one political banner. As is natural in so large a group, nearly every shade of political faith is represented.

A large proportion of the young people who come to the settlements are attracted to the independent political movements, and are likely to respond to appeals to their civic conscience. While serving on a State Commission I heard an upstate colleague repeat the rumor that Governor Hughes, then a candidate for re-election, was to be knifed by his party. We had seen in our section of the city no active campaign on his behalf. Posters, pictures, and flattering references were conspicuously absent. Governor Hughes had made a profound impression upon all but the advocates of rigid party control because of his high-minded integrity and emancipation from "practical" political methods. I telephoned two or three of our young men that the time seemed ripe for some action in our neighborhood. In an incredibly short time a small group of Democrats, Republicans, and Socialists gathered in the sitting-room of the Henry Street house, and within twenty-four hours an Independent League was formed to bring the Governor's candidacy before the neighborhood. Financial and moral support came from other friends, and before the end of the week he addressed in Clinton Hall an enthusiastic mass-meeting organized by this league without help from the members of his own political organization.

The sporadic attempts of good citizens to organize for reform have, I am sure, given practical politicians food for merriment. One election night, dispirited because of the defeat of an upright and able man, I was about to enter the settlement when one of the district leaders said: " Your friends don't play the game intelligently. You telephone them *to-night* to begin to organize if they want to beat us next election. You got to begin early and stick to it."

However, every sincere reform campaign is valuable because of its immediate and far-reaching educational effect, even when the candidates fail of election. It is gratifying to those who are socially interested to watch the evolution of political platforms. Every party now inserts human welfare planks and pledges devotion to measures that in the days of our initiation were regarded as dreams and ridiculed as beyond the realm of practicality. Settlements have increasing authority because of the persistency of their interest in social welfare measures. They accumulate in their daily routine significant facts obtainable in no other way. Governors and legislators listen, and sooner or later act on the representations of responsible advocates whose facts are current and trustworthy. The experience of the social worker is often utilized by the state. At the twentieth anniversary of our settlement the Mayor drew public attention to the fact that no less than five important city departments were intrusted to men and one woman who were qualified for public duty by administration of or long-continued association with the settlements.

Soon after our removal to Henry Street in 1895 messengers from the " Association," the important political club of the district, brought lanterns and flags with which we were requested to decorate in honor of a clambake to be given the next day. The event had been glaringly and expensively advertised for some time. The marchers were to pass our house in the morning and on their return in the evening. The young men glowed with the excitement of their recital, and I can still see the blank look of non-comprehension that passed over their faces when I tried to soften refusal by explaining—lamely, I fear—our reasons for avoiding the implications of participation. The courteous district leader of the other great party was equally at sea when, a short time after, he brought flags and decorations for their more humble celebration and met with the same refusal. The immediate conclusion appeared to be that we were enemies or " reformers," and the charge was held against us.

The gay and spirited clambake parade, with its bands and flying banners, the shooting rockets and loud applause of the friends of the marchers, had passed by when we were drawn to the windows to gaze upon another procession. Straggling, unkempt, dispirited-looking marchers returned our scrutiny and held aloft a banner bearing the legend " Socialist Labor Party," the portrait of a man, and beneath it the name " Daniel De Leon."

It was our first intimation of the socialist movement in America, and students of its history will be able to identify this leader and recall the pioneer part he played in its early phases, his alliance with the once-powerful Knights of Labor, and the progress and decline of his society now overshadowed by the present Socialist Party.[1]

Meeting a neighbor on the Bowery one day about two years later, he stopped to explain that he was on his way to an interesting performance, and invited me to accompany him. Together we walked along until we reached the Thalia Theater, famous under its old name of the Bowery in the annals of the American stage. In this theater Charlotte Cushman made her first appearance in New York, and here the elder Booth, Lester Wallack, and other great players delighted the theatergoers of their day.

Venders of suspenders, hot sausages, and plaster statuettes surrounded the building, and placards on the Greek columns advertised the event as " The Spoken Newspaper." A huge audience was listening to editorials and special articles read by the authors themselves, and the atmosphere was charged with intense purpose. Acquaintances gathered quickly, and eagerly explained to me that members of labor organizations and " intellectuals " of the neighborhood

[1] See "History of Socialism in the United States," by Morris Hillquit (Funk and Wagnalls).

had united for the purpose of publishing a newspaper for socialist propaganda and to help the
cause of the working classes. They had little
money; in fact, were in debt. The men had
contributed from their scanty wages; those who
possessed watches had pawned them, and they
were using this medium (" The Spoken Newspaper ") to raise money to pay the printer and
other clamorous creditors, a charge of ten cents
being made for admission to the theater. A
charter had been obtained under the name of
" The Forward Association," but I was made to
understand that this was not a stock corpora-
tion and was not organized for profit.

The genuinely social purpose of the organization held the men together during the lean
years that were to follow. Finally, in 1908, the
Association became self-supporting, and in 1911
the charter was amended to meet the enormously extended field. The Forward Association now publishes a daily paper in Yiddish,
with a regular circulation of 177,000, and a
monthly periodical, and holds property estimated to be worth half a million dollars. From
its funds it has aided struggling propagandist
newspapers and has given help to labor organizations.

The hope of a more equal distribution of
wealth bites early into the consciousness of the

proletariat. Even the children, who cannot be excluded from any discussion in a tenement home, have opinions on the subject. Happening one day upon a club of youngsters, I interrupted a fiery debate on socialism. Its twelve-year-old defender presented his argument in this fashion: " You see, gentlemen, it's this way: The millionaires sit round the table eating sponge-cake and the bakers are down in the cellars baking it. But the day will come,"— and here the young orator pointed an accusing finger at the universe—" when the bakers will come up from their cellars and say, ' Gentlemen, bake your own sponge-cake.' "

Mixed with my admiration for the impressive oratory was the guilty sense that the settlement was probably responsible for the picture of licentious living manifested by the consumption of sponge-cake,—our most popular refreshment, with ice cream added on great occasions.

However one may question the party socialists' claim that an economic and social millennium is exclusively dependent upon their dominance, few acquainted with those active in the movement will deny the sincerity of purpose, the almost religious exaltation that animate great numbers of the party. The first socialist member from the East, and the second in the

United States, has been elected to Congress from our district; a man universally esteemed for his probity, with a record of many years' unselfish devotion to the workingmen's cause.

A copious literature and widespread propaganda proclaim the willingness of the American people now to give socialism a hearing. It seems a far cry from that first unimpressive little parade that drew the settlement family to the windows twenty years ago.

Years ago the lads in one of the settlement clubs debating the subject of woman suffrage declared it to be " a well-known fact that when women had the vote they cut off their hair, they donned men's attire; their voices became harsh."

I cannot say that even to-day the ardent advocates of woman suffrage come in great numbers from among the male members of the settlement clubs, but, on the whole, the tendency is to accept women in politics as a necessary phase of this transitional period and the readjustment of the old relations. The conviction that the extension of democracy should include women has found free expression in our part of the city, and Miss L. L. Dock, a resident of many years, has mobilized Russians, Italians,

Irish, and native-born, all the nationalities of our cosmopolitan community, for the campaign. When the suffrage parade marched down Fifth Avenue in 1913, back of the settlement banner, with its symbol of universal brotherhood, there walked a goodly company carrying flags with the suffrage demand in ten languages. The cosmopolitanism of our district was marked by the Sephardic Jewish girl who bore aloft the Turkish appeal. The Chinese banner was made by a Chinese physician and a Chinese missionary. There are four American-born Chinese voters in our part of the city.

The transition is significant from the position of women among orthodox Jews to the motherly looking woman who stands on a soapbox at the corner of Henry Street and makes her appeal for the franchise to a respectful

group of laboring men. The mere fact that this "mother in Israel" is obliged to work in a factory six days of the week is an argument in itself, but intelligently and interestingly she develops her plea, and her appeal to the men's reason brings sober nods of approval.

The Russian revolution owes much to the valorous women who from the formation of the Tschaikowsky circles in the early '70s have worked as comrades for the cause, and this is well known to the "intellectuals" of the East Side. I doubt whether a single man or woman could be found among them opposed to granting the franchise to women. If they seem indifferent, it is doubtless because they think it a matter of course and strenuous effort to secure votes for women unnecessary. From the party organization men there is not so much encouragement.

Commissioner of Corrections Katherine Davis testifies that the inmates of the girls' reformatory disapprove of women voting as "unladylike," and it may surprise those who do not know the thought of these poor women to learn that they cling to orthodox ideals. I understand that I shocked one girl, who had been sentenced to the "Island" from the Night Court, by advocating the appointment of women police. The probation officer who called upon

A Mother in Israel

her asked her opinion of my recommendation, which was then sufficiently novel to attract newspaper attention. " Oh," said the girl, " it's not right. Woman's place is the home."

CHAPTER XV

SOCIAL FORCES, Continued

THE drama is taken seriously in our neighborhood, particularly among the people whose taste has not been affected by familiarity with plays or theaters classed as typically "American." In the years of our residence on the East Side there have been several transitions in the Yiddish drama [1] from classic to modern and realistic. Feeling has at times run high between the advocates of the different schools, and discussions in the press and disputes in the cafés have reflected a very lively popular interest.

Jacob Gordin, the Yiddish playwright, contributed an important chapter to the history of the stage, and his art was, I think, a factor in drawing intelligent attention to the East Side.

[1] The early Hebrews possessed a few mystery plays, " The Sale of Joseph," " Esther and Haman," and " David and Goliath," and at the Jewish carnival of Purim (Feast of Esther) merrymakers went from house to house giving performances of song and mimicry, but the Yiddish theater is new and was first introduced in Rumania not more than thirty-five years ago. Transplanted to Russia, the actors, said to have been selected from the original strolling companies, played a brilliant brief part until, under government order, the Yiddish theaters were closed there.

The Yiddish drama, before his time, had not been looked upon with great favor, and there was in this, as in other instances, an implication of the contempt that Americans not infrequently feel for the alien, and also a fear, on the part of members of the older Jewish communities, that the Yiddish theater might retard the Americanization of the immigrant.

Mr. Gordin was one of our early friends, and we found pleasure in our theater parties. The audiences seemed scarcely less dramatic than the performers, and we took sides, perhaps not illogically, with the new school. Upon our appearance interpreters from various parts of the house were sure to offer their kind services. The acting was of high grade, and the fame of some of the performers has now gone far beyond the neighborhood and the city. The stage during this period performed its time-honored function of teaching and moralizing. One of Gordin's plays that had many seasons of popularity was "The Jewish King Lear." It depicted the endless clashing between the generations. The Shakespearean Cordelia, on the Bowery stage, is the daughter of character who longs for self-expression and becomes a physician. Another impressive play was "God, Man, and the Devil." Here was preached the story of man's fall, not because of poverty, but through the possession of riches. The pious Jewish scribe resists the worldly man and his enticements, but having come into the possession of money he becomes grasping, eager for power, susceptible to flattery. The portrayal of his spiritual downfall gave the playwright opportunity for remarkable delineation of Jewish character. I also found it interesting to take William Archer, the English critic, on his first visit to America, to see Ibsen metamorphosed in " The Jewish Nora," which was then playing at a nearby theater.

The Italians have now almost abandoned the marionette theater, and we can no longer find on Mott, Elizabeth, and Spring Streets the stuffy little theaters filled with workingmen (and an occasional woman), sitting enthralled night after night while from the wings the fine voice of the reader continued the story of Rinaldo and other popular knights.

The puppet theater was usually a family affair. Its members slept and cooked behind the scenes, alternating in reading the story or operating the puppet figures of knights and ladies. One hot night we strolled from the settlement to a marionette theater nearby to show our guests (among them a theatrical producer) the simplicity of the primitive stage still to be found in the great city.

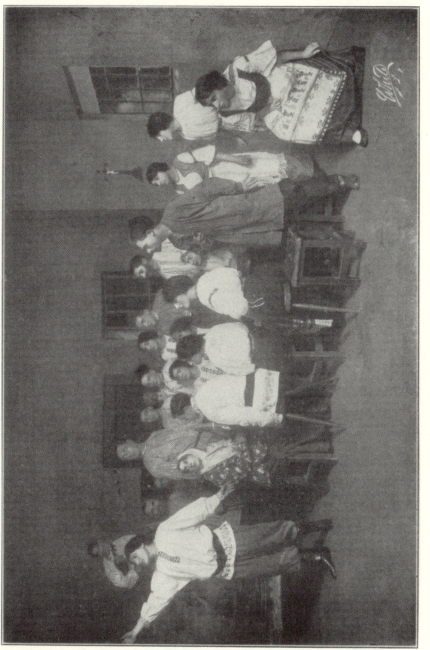

The Dramatic Club Presented "The Shepherd"

During the story that was then being enacted a doll, representing the infant heir, was dropped in a miniature forest to be rescued by the valorous knight. At that moment the naked baby of the proprietor walked out from the wings, crossed the stage, and snatching up the doll, clasped it tight in her little arms and disappeared. The audience gave no sign that the current of their enchantment had been broken, nor did the reader or the manipulator of the rescuing knight pause for a second in their roles.

The theaters on the Bowery and in its vicinity advertise Italian opera and occasional revivals of serious drama, but more obvious at present are the lurid advertisements of sensational melodrama. We are plainly under the influence of Broadway and the " movies," but at the Metropolitan Opera House our neighbors can always be seen in great numbers among the " appreciators " at the top of the house.

A short time ago an unselfish and well-beloved member of the older circle of Russian revolutionists asked me to help him establish a comrade on some self-supporting basis, and began by saying, " Being a literary man, he wants to open a restaurant." The fact of his being " literary " would immediately bring him custom, and I foresaw another meeting-place for philosophers, poets, and revolutionists, graduates of universities or gymnasia, writers and publicists, students familiar with Kant and Comte and Spinoza.

In these little East Side cafes, over a steam-ing glass of tea or a temperate meal, endless discussions take place. In the groups that gather there are many men of education who, during their first years in this country, worked as cloakmakers, tailors, or factory operatives until they were able to obtain employment more suited to their aptitudes or talents.

The cafés and the bookshop where the interesting proprietor specializes in radical literature are the meeting-places for the "intellectuals," centers from which radiate influences that are not insignificant. As they prosper, many of these men move their families to other parts of the city, but they continue to be East Siders at heart, and find congenial atmosphere in their old haunts. So they come back for the fellowship they miss in their new habitations.

The saloons of the neighborhood touch the life of an entirely different set. They are informal club-houses for many men, some of whom have for years been members of the same political organization. Not that the organization trusts to the saloon alone. All through our neighborhood are the club-houses maintained for members of the party who are kept together through social intercourse.

However, among workingmen, the saloon may be patronized for other reasons than refreshment and sociability. When I expressed to a sober man, long out of work, my surprise that he should have been seen going into a saloon, he explained that if a man did not sometimes go there he was likely to be out of work a longer time. "The fellows just kind of talk about jobs when they're sittin' round in the saloons, and sometimes you pick up something." His reasoning reminded me of a friend who professed indifference to the numerous expensive clubs to which he belonged, but found them useful in his business. "Often a chance conversation or a meeting with men develops into something big."

When the Empress of Austria was assassinated in 1898 newspaper reporters, seeking "color," asked the settlement's direction to anarchists who, in the excitement of the time, were believed to form a considerable portion of the East Side population.

I recalled two men who, in a cellar in Grand Street, had a few rows of books for sale which advertised them as "Dealers in Radical Literature." One partner proclaimed himself a State Socialist, the other a Philosophic Anarchist. The latter, mild and gentle, devoted disciple of Prudhon, with whose writings he was familiar, was almost pathetically grateful, and showed not altogether complimentary surprise when we purchased Kropotkin's "Fields, Factories, and Workshops," Tolstoi's "My Life," and Walt Whitman's poems. In his naïve simplicity he assumed that only those unsure of food and shelter found interest in such literature, and later he and his partner, in all seriousness, proposed, with our co-operation, to reform society.

They had decided, after much thought, that the reason the people they met at the settlement seemed to sympathize and understand was because of the books they read. They felt sorry for the people on Fifth Avenue who, living so far away from the poor, could not know how things might be remedied. Their plan was that I should rent a store opening on the avenue, place comfortable chairs and tables upon which books could be spread. These books the merchants would loan,—their whole stock, if necessary,—and then people passing on foot or driving by could stop and read.

Such naïvete could hardly be met with to-day, for education and discussion of themes of social interest have widened the minds of the community and contact with people of different positions in life is much more general.

Police interference with free speech and free assemblage in our country has stirred vigorous protest from sober people and has had the effect of kindling enthusiasm for propaganda of ultraradical philosophies among those who might otherwise never have given thought to them. In some quarters mere radicalism has become perilously popular. The spirit of adventure, a kind of generous devotion not always balanced with knowledge of definite issues or the constructive processes that are under way, deflect forces that might be employed for immediate advances in social welfare.

I recall the indignation of a young man, just graduated from one of our universities, when chance took him into an East Side hall where a well-known anarchist was addressing a large and attentive audience and reading selections from Thoreau. Without any obvious provocation the police jumped upon the platform, arrested the woman and those who sat with her, refused them permission to call a cab, and drove them in the patrol wagon to the police station. At the time there was no limit to which this man would not have gone to show his resentment against the injustice of the proceeding, and it was some relief to his chivalrous spirit to testify against the police and to use the settlement's experience in giving publicity to the occurrence.

Something of this menace to cherished American institutions lay in the occurrences at Lawrence, Massachusetts, during the winter of 1912.

Unsatisfactory labor conditions gave the Industrial Workers of the World an opportunity to capture the loyalty and devotion of the discontented operatives. Reports of the unwarranted action of police and militia during a strike that ensued, the imprisonment of the strike leaders, and the difficulty of securing for them an impartial hearing were incidents too serious to be lightly dismissed from the mind. I went to Lawrence at that time, and came away reflecting with sadness on the manifestations there of how slight is our hold upon civilization, how insecure our reliance upon the courts for justice when feelings run high.

The operatives' story had not reached the

general public, and I offered the House on Henry Street as one medium for informing people in New York who had no link with the working people.

A participant in the strike came to us to tell the story, and her presentation, on the whole, seemed fair and reasonable. It was no less an indictment of the leaders of the established labor organizations for failure to unionize the workers, and thereby secure better wages and shorter hours, than of the capitalist, who, the speaker thought, should be held responsible for creating the conditions.

The reaction of the audience was definite— that the workers should have tangible assurance of the existence of an American sentiment for justice, and money came spontaneously to the settlement to be sent to the strikers and toward the cost of the defense of the prisoners. The New York press, on the whole, gave fair interpretation of the causes of discontent and the disturbing consequences to society of what appeared to some observers to be anarchistic methods on the part of those in authority.

The Social Reform Club, organized in 1894, was a factor in helping to stimulate a more general public interest in matters of social concern.

The club aimed at the immediate future, and labored solely for measures that had a fair promise of early success. Its members, wage-earners and non-wage-earners in almost equal numbers, were required to have " a deep active interest in the elevation of society, especially by the improvement of the condition of wage-earners."

Ernest Crosby, Tolstoian and reformer, was the first president, and the original membership comprised distinguished men and women, courageous thinkers who fully met the requirements of the society, and others, like myself, who were to gain enlightenment regarding methods and theories for the direct improvement of industrial and social conditions.

Father Ducey, whose support of Father McGlynn[1] during his time of trial was then still referred to; Charles B. Spahr, and others no longer living were among the organizers. On the club's weekly programmes can be read the names of men and women who were then and still are bearers of light for the community. Devoted members of the club testified to their

---

[1] Dr. Edward McGlynn was suspended in 1884 under charge of advocacy of Henry George and of holding opinions regarding the rights of property not in accord with Catholic teaching, and later excommunicated. He organized the famous Anti-Poverty Society in 1887. In 1892 he was reinstated, his position being judged not contrary to the doctrine of the Church as confirmed by the Encyclical *Rerum Novarum* issued by Leo XIII on May 15, 1891.

indebtedness to the Knights of Labor as "a great educational force for social reform," and a younger generation gained immeasurably from association with men and women who had given themselves unselfishly to the early labor movements in this country.

It was at the time of excessive sweatshop abuses, and from the windows of our tenement home we could look upon figures bent over the whirring foot-power machines. One room in particular almost unnerved us. Never did we go to bed so late or rise so early that we saw the machines at rest, and the unpleasant conditions where manufacturing was carried on in the overcrowded rooms of the families we nursed disquieted us more than the diseases we were trying to combat.

Our sympathies were ready for enlistment when working people whom we knew, and whose sobriety of habits and mind won confidence and esteem, discussed the possibility of improving conditions through organization. In another place I have told how the young girls first led us into the trades union movement, but now where the standard of the entire family was involved through the wage and working conditions of its chief wage-earner, it became to us a movement of greater significance.

We were accorded a doubtful distinction by

acquaintances who had no point of contact with working people when we acknowledged friendship with "demagogues" and "walking delegates" (terms which they used interchangeably), and, inexperienced though we were, it was possible for us, in a small way, to help build a bridge of understanding.

Research was not then a popular expression of social interest. Discussions developed the need of a formal investigation into conditions, and a distinguished economist of Yale was asked to send someone academic and "without feeling for either side," while we chose a labor leader, well informed from the workers' point of view, to make the inquiry. The paraphernalia of cards, filing cabinets, et cetera, was provided, and a room set apart in the settlement, but the investigation ended before it was fairly begun with mutual scorn on the part of the two men.

Through the years that have followed the settlement has from time to time been the neutral ground where both sides might meet, or has furnished the "impartial third party" in industrial disputes.

One such conference lingers in my memory because of the open-mindedness shown by a man whose traditions and training were far removed from wage-earners' problems. A friend and generously interested in all our undertakings, he questioned my judgment in espousing the workingmen's side in a threatened strike, believing that a compromise on disputed hours and pay during that unprosperous time was better than interrupted employment. We believed that the "half loaf" might prove too costly. The wage was already below a living minimum, and the workers' contention that at the beginning of the season the market could be made to meet a fair charge for labor seemed to us an entirely reasonable one. My friend agreed to bring representatives of the manufacturers and contractors if I would bring an equal number of workers to a conference in the Henry Street house, over which he would preside. No agreement was reached, but when the strike was finally declared this friend, whose wisdom and experience have placed him high in the councils of the nation, had come to see that the workers could not do otherwise, and throughout the strike he aided with money and sympathy.

Since those days cloaks are no longer made in New York tenement homes, and the once unhappy, sweated workers, united with other garment-makers, have been lifted into eminence because of the unusual character of their organization.

In 1910, after a prolonged strike, peace was declared under a " protocol," [1] wherein were combined unique methods devised for the control of shops and adjustment of difficulties between the association of progressive manufacturers and the trades unions. New terms—" a preferential union shop " and the " Joint Board of Sanitary Control "—were introduced. Under the latter, for the first time in the history of industry, sanitary standards were enforced by the trade itself. On this board, the expense of which was shared equally by the association of manufacturers and the trades unions, were representatives of both organizations, their attorneys, and three representatives of the public unanimously elected by both parties to the agreement.

When I was asked to be one of the three representatives of the public, already laden with responsibilities I was loath to accept another, but the temptation to have even a small share in the socializing of industries involving in New York City alone nearly 100,000 people and several hundred millions of dollars was irresistible.

High sanitary standards and a living wage,

[1] See reports and bulletins of the Joint Board of Sanitary Control (Dr. George Price, Director), also Bulletins Nos. 98, 144, 145, and 146 of the U. S. Department of Labor, and " Sanitary Control of an Industry by Itself," by L. D. Wald, in the report of the International Congress of Hygiene and Demography, 1913.

with reasonable hours of employment, were assured so long as both parties submitted to the terms of the protocol. Whatever changes in the administration of the trade agreement may be made, the protocol has established certain principles invaluable for the present and for future negotiations. The world seemed to have moved since we shuddered over the long hours and the germ-exposed garments in the tenements.[1]

[1] In August, 1915, the protocol was succeeded by a time agreement of two years. This agreement contains the main principles of the protocol, with some modifications in the machinery of adjustment.

CHAPTER XVI

NEW AMERICANS AND OUR POLICIES

ILLUMINATING anecdotes might be told of the storm and stress that often lie beneath the surface of the immigrant's experience from the time he purchases his ticket in the old country until the gates at Ellis Island close behind him  and the process of assimilation begins. That he has so often been left rudderless in strange seas forms a chapter in the history of this " land of opportunity " that cannot be omitted.

The confusion of the stranger, unable to speak the language and encountering unfamiliar laws and institutions, often has tragic results. Once in searching for a patient in a large tenement near the Bowery I knocked at each door in turn. An Italian woman hesitatingly opened one, no wider than to give me a glimpse of a slight creature obviously stricken with fear. Her face brought instantly to my mind the famous picture of the sorrowing mother. "Dolorosa!" I said. The tone and the word sufficed, and she opened the door wide enough to let me enter. In a corner of the room lay two children with marks of starvation upon them.

Laying my hat and bag upon the table, to indicate that I would return, I flew to the nearest grocery for food, taking time, while my purchases were being made ready, to telephone to a distinguished Italian upon whose interest and sympathy I could rely to meet me at the tenement, that we might learn the cause of this obvious distress.

My friend arrived before I had finished feeding the children, and to him the little mother poured forth her tale. She, with three children, had arrived some days before, to meet the husband who had preceded her and had prepared the home for them. One *bambina* was ill when they reached port, and it was taken from her, why she could not explain. She was allowed to land with the other two and join her husband, and the following day, in answer to their frantic inquiries, they learned that the child had been taken to a hospital and had died there. Then her husband was arrested, and she, unacquainted with a single human being in the city, found herself alone with two starving children, too frightened to open the door or to venture upon the street. She thought her husband was imprisoned somewhere nearby.

My friend and I went together to the Ludlow Street jail, and here a curious thing occurred. We merely inquired for the prisoner; we asked no questions. His cell door was opened and he was released. Later I learned that he had been arrested because of failure to make a satisfactory payment on a watch he was buying on the installment plan. There must have been gross irregularity in the transaction, judging by the willingness to release him and the fact that his creditor failed to appear against him. It was hinted, at the time, that there was collusion between the installment plan dealers and the prison officials.

A pleasanter story is that of the B—— family. One evening two neighborhood women, shawls over their heads, called to ask if I would contribute to a fund they were raising to furnish quarters for a family just arrived from Ellis Island. When I expressed wonder that they should have been permitted to land in a penniless condition the women shrugged their shoulders in characteristic fashion and said, " Well, they're here, and we must do something."

Not wishing to refuse, or to participate blindly, I asked for the whereabouts of the man of the family. I found him in a basement, a very dignified, gray-haired cobbler, between 40 and 45 years of age. When I asked how it happened that the first step of his family in America should be to claim help in this way he explained the complications in which they had been involved. He had preceded his family to make a home for them, and after some years had sent money for steamer tickets for them. When they arrived at  the frontier, owing to some technicality, they were sent back. He had sent more money to defray the additional expenses; then himself had been compelled to undergo an operation for appendicitis, which took all he had hoarded to furnish the home. He was just out of the hospital when wife and children arrived.

Appreciating the importance of having the family begin life in their new environment with dignity and self-respect, an offer was made to loan him money if he would recall the women who were begging for him. Together we figured out the minimum sum needed, and within an hour the twenty-five dollars was in his hands and he had recalled the women with joy. He took the loan without exaggerated protest or gratitude, merely saying: " As there is a God in heaven you will not regret this."

He was a skillful cobbler and the wife a good housekeeper, and in six months they brought back the twenty-five dollars. It was pleasanter not to think of the pinching in the household that made this prompt repayment possible. Some time later he brought me forty dollars which the family had saved, saying he knew it would give me pleasure to start the savings-bank account which they would need for the education of the children. The subsequent history of this family, like many another known to us in Henry Street, shows the real contribution brought into American life by immigrants of this character.

In discussions throughout the country of the problems of immigration it is significant that few, if any, of the men and women who have had extended opportunity for social contact with the foreigner favor a further restriction of immigration.

The government's policy regarding the immigrant has been negative, concerned with exclusion and deportation, with the head tax and the enforcement of treaties and international

agreements. By our laws we are protected from the pauper, the sick, and the vicious; but only within recent years has a hearing been given to those who have asked that our government assume an affirmative policy of protection, distribution, and assimilation.

The need of constructive social measures has long been indicated. The planting of roots in the new soil can best be accomplished through an intercourse with the immigrant in which the dignity of the individual and of the family is recognized. Heroic measures may be necessary to establish a satisfactory system of distribution, and these measures must be based on a philosophic understanding of democracy. Among them should be provision for giving instruction to the prospective immigrant in regard to those laws, customs, or prohibitions with which he is liable to come in contact, and also in regard to the industrial opportunities open to him. Then, with competent medical examination at the port of departure and humane consideration there and here, the tragedies now so frequent at the port of arrival might be diminished, or even eliminated altogether.

In turn, the private banker, the employment agent, the ticket broker, the lawyer, and the notary public have battened upon the helplessness of the immigrant. Our experience has convinced us that in the interest of the state itself the future citizens should be made to feel that protection and fair treatment are accorded by the state. The greater number of immigrants who come to us are adults for whose upbringing this country has been at no expense. It would seem only just to give them special protection during their first years in the country, to encourage confidence in our institutions, and to promote assimilation. From an academic point of view, it might be said that all institutions for the citizen are available to the immigrant, but the statement carries with it an implication of equal ability on the part of the latter to utilize these institutions, and this is not borne out by the experience of those familiar with actual conditions.

Such thoughts as these lay back of an invitation to Governor Hughes to dine and spend an evening at the settlement and there meet the colleagues who could speak with authority on these matters.

The Governor left us armed with maps and documentary evidence. A few months later the legislature authorized the creation of a commission to " make full inquiry, examination, and investigation into the condition, welfare, and industrial opportunities of aliens in the State of New York." Among its nine members were two women, Frances Kellor and myself. Upon the recommendation of that commission the New York Bureau of Industries and Immigration of the Department of Labor was created.[1]

[1] Report of Commission on Immigration of the State of New York transmitted to the legislature in April, 1909.

Miss Kellor, the first woman to be head of a state bureau, became its chief.

Pending the enactment of legislation, she and I, with a photographer and a sympathetic companion interested in questions of labor, motored over the state examining the construction camps of the barge canal (a state contract), the camps connected with the city's great new aqueduct, and some of the canning establishments.

In the latter we found ample illustration of indifference on the part of private employers. In the camps surrounding the canneries were large numbers of idle children who should have been in school. The local authorities were, perhaps not unnaturally, indisposed to enforce the compulsory education law upon these children whose stay in the community was to be a transient one. In the public work the New York City contracts, with few exceptions, showed carefully thought-out and standardized conditions for the men; but examination of the state contracts showed that while elaborate provision had been made for the expert handling of every other detail connected with the work, even to the stabling of the mules, nowhere was any mention made of the men.

In a shack that held three tiers of bunks, occupied alternately by the day and night

shifts, with a cook-stove in a little clearing in
the middle, we found a homesick man, who
chanced not to be on the works, reading a book.
When we engaged in conversation with him
he pointed contemptuously to the bunks and
their dirty coverings, and said, " This Amer-

ica! I show you Rome," and produced from
under his bed a photograph of the Coliseum.

The commission exposed many forms of exploitation of the immigrant, and subsequent
reports have corroborated its findings. Some
safeguards have now been established, and the
reports of the Bureau of Industries and Immigration in the first years of its existence bore
interesting testimony to its practical and social
value. The significance of the indifference of
the state to its employees, as it appeared to the

investigators, was given publicity at the time, and roused comment and discussion. I quote from it as follows:

" The state, as employer, alone determines the terms upon which its new canal shall be built. It defines in great detail its standard of materials and workmanship, but takes no thought for the workmen who must operate in great transient groups. It does not leave to chance the realization of its material standard, but sends inspectors to make tests and provides a staff of engineers. It does leave to chance (in the ignorance and cupidity of *padroni*) the quality and price of foods and care of the men. It takes great care to prevent the freezing of cement, but permits any kind of houses to be used for its laborers. It is wholly indifferent as to how they are ventilated, lighted, or heated, how many men sleep in them, or whether the sleeping quarters are also used for cooking and eating and the bunks as cupboards. Neither does it care whether the men can keep themselves or their clothes clean.

" The simplest standards which military history shows are essential in handling such artificial bodies of people are grossly violated. Sanitary conveniences are sometimes entirely omitted; the men drink any kind of water they can obtain, and filthy grounds are of no evident concern. The state does not inquire whether there are hospitals or physicians, medicine, emergency aids, or anything of the kind. Notice is taken of gambling, drunkenness, and immorality only when they impair the efficiency of the men. . . . Men left alone in these miserable, uninspected shacks, where vermin and dirt prevail . . . must inevitably deteriorate. The testimony of contractors themselves is that many of the laborers become nomads, drifting from camp to camp, drinking, quarreling, and averse to steady work.

"We commend this responsibility in all its phases to the various state departments charged with education, health, letting of contracts, payment of bills, supervision of highways and waterways, and protection of laborers. We ask the state as employer to consider its gain from the men at the most productive periods of their lives; we ask the state to measure the influence of this life upon its future citizens during their first years in the country when they are most receptive to impressions of America."[1]

Quite recently the Public Health Council of the New York State Department of Health has adopted a sanitary code for all labor camps.

It is impossible to compute the sums that

[1] "The Construction Camps of the People," by Lillian D. Wald and Frances A. Kellor (*The Survey,* January 1, 1910).

have been lost by immigrants through fake
banks, fake express companies, and irresponsible
steamship agencies. In New York State these
were practically legislated out of existence
through the efforts of the Commission of Immigration of 1909 just referred to, yet in the
winter of 1914-15 approximately $12,000,000
was lost on the lower East Side by the failure
of private banks, sweeping away the savings
and capital of between 60,000 and 70,000 depositors. Happily, the postal savings bank has
come, and is already much used by immigrants,
incidentally keeping a large amount of money in
this country. In important centers the stations
might be socialized to the still greater advantage of the depositors and the service by having
someone assigned to interpret, to write addresses and give information. These favors
have been the bait held out to the timid
stranger by the private agencies.

Perhaps an even greater loss has come to us
through the land-sale deceptions. Farms cultivated in New York State are actually decreas-
ing, while the population increases. The census
of 1900-1910 shows 4.9 per cent. decrease of
farms and 25.4 per cent. increase of population.
Great numbers of the immigrants are peasants,
and land-hungry, and if there was a policy
throughout the states of registration of land for

A Region of Overcrowded Homes

prospective settlers, and if severe penalties attached to land frauds, I have little doubt that valuable workers might be directed to the enormous areas that need cultivation. "I am an agriculturist," said a man who found his way to the settlement to tell his troubles, "and I pull out nails in a box factory in New York." His entire family have followed him to the land that he is now cultivating.

One winter a number of peasants from the Baltic provinces found themselves stranded in New York. It was a period of unemployment, and they could find no work. Unaccustomed to cities, they eagerly seized upon an opportunity to leave New York. At the settlement, where they were assembled, a state official told them of wood-cutters needed—in Herkimer County, as I remember it. An advertisement called for forty men, and the responsibility of the advertiser was vouched for by the local banker.

"Who can cut trees?" I asked. A shout went up from these countrymen—"Who cannot cut trees?" *Forty* to go? Everyone was ready. So we financed them in their quest for work, and bade good-by to a radiant, grateful group. *Alas! only four men were needed.* The contractor preferred to have a larger number come, that he might make selection. And this

is not an exceptional instance. Ask the itinerant workers, the tramps even, how much faith
can be placed in the advertisements of " Hands
Wanted " in the East and in the West at the
gathering of the crops.

The possibility of deflecting people to the
land has been demonstrated by Jewish societies
in New York, and with proper support other
organizations interested in this phase of the
immigrant's welfare might repeat their success.
Such programmes of distribution, however, cannot be carried out without effective co-operation from the people in the rural regions,
and assimilative processes will not be wholly
successful until the native-born American is
freed from some of his prejudices and provin-
cialism.

An unsocial attitude in the country naturally
drives the stranger to an intensive colony life
which accentuates the disadvantages of the barriers he and we build up.

An experience in Westchester County illustrates this very well. We were seeking lodgings
for two intelligent and attractive young Italians
who were working on a dam at one of our settlement country places. Incidentally, the work
they were doing was quite beyond the powers
of any native workers in the vicinity of whom
we could hear. We asked an old native couple,

squatters on some adjacent land, to rent an unoccupied floor of their house to the two young
men. The man, despite their extremely indigent
condition (the wife went to the almshouse a
short time after), absolutely refused, fearing the
loss of social prestige if they " lived in the
house with dagoes."

Perhaps, having little else, they were justified
in clinging to their social exclusiveness, but
their action in this case illustrates the almost
universal attitude toward the immigrant, particularly the more recent ones, and perhaps
only those who have felt the isolation and lone-
liness of the newcomer can comprehend its
cruelty.

An educated Chinese merchant who once
called at the settlement apologized for the
eagerness with which he accepted an offer to
show him over the house, explaining that although he had been thirty years in this country
ours was the first American home he had been
invited to enter.

We need also to analyze the philosophy of
much of the discrimination against aliens in the
matter of employment, and it is not pleasant
to remember that until recently a state employing an enormous number of foreign workers
forbade the bringing of suit by the non-resident
family of the alien, although he might have

lost his life in an accident through no fault of his own.

Scorn of the immigrant is not peculiar to our generation. A search of old newspaper files will show that the arrival of great numbers of immigrants of any one nationality has always been considered a problem. In turn each nationality as it became established in the new country has considered the next-comers a danger. The early history of Pennsylvania records the hostility to the Germans—" fear dominated the minds of the Colonists "—despite the fact that the German invaders were land-owning and good farmers.

An Irish boy observed to one of our residents that on Easter Day he intended to kill his little Jewish classmate. Having had long experience of the vigorous language and kind heart of the young Celt, she paid little attention to the threat, but was more startled when the soft-eyed Francesco chimed in that he was also going to destroy him " because he killed my Gawd." " But," said the teacher, " Christ was a Jew." " Yes, I know," answered the young defender of the faith, " He was then, but He's an American now."

Despite its absurdity, was not the boy's conception an exaggerated illustration of that surface patriotism which is almost universally stimulated and out of which soul-deadening prejudices may grow—may take root even in the public schools?

Great is our loss when a shallow Americanism is accepted by the newly arrived immigrant, more particularly by the children, and their national traditions and heroes are ruthlessly pushed aside. The young people have usually to be urged by someone outside their own group to recognize the importance and value of customs, and even of ethical teaching, when given in a foreign language, or by old-world people with whom the new American does not wish to be associated in the minds of his acquaintances. This does not apply only to the recent immigrant, to whom his children often hear contemptuous terms applied. I remember attending a public hearing before the Department of Education of New York City at which Germans vigorously urged the study of their native tongue in the public schools, because of the impossibility of persuading their children to learn or use the language by any other means than that of having it made a part of the great American public school system.

It is difficult to find evidence of any serious effort on our part to comprehend the mental reaction upon the immigrant of the American institutions he encounters. Indeed, gathering up the story of the immigrant, I sometimes wonder if he, like the fairies, does not hold up a magic mirror wherein our social ethics are reflected, rather than his own visage.

What we are to the immigrant in our civic, social, and ethical relations is quite as important as what he is to us. We risk destruction of the spirit—that element of life that makes it human—when we disregard our neighbor's personality.

Recent discussion of immigration bills focuses attention on two points deemed of fundamental importance by the settlement groups.

Three Presidents have vetoed bills for the restriction of immigration by means of a literacy test or by conditions that would virtually deny the right of asylum for political refugees. Once, in addressing a committee of the House on such proposed legislation, I protested against a departure from our tradition and reminded the members of the committee of the splendid Americans who would have been lost to this country had the door been so closed upon them. A young physician of Polish parentage followed, and his cultured diction and attractive appearance lent emphasis to his story. " My father," he said, " came an illiterate to this country because the priest of his parish happened not to be interested in education, not because my father was indifferent. He has struggled all his life to give his children what he himself could never have, and has worshiped the country that gave us opportunity."

In his veto of the bill President Wilson admirably formulated his reasons for opposing restriction of this character, and as these are exactly the arguments upon which social workers have based their objections, I cannot do better than quote him here:

" In two particulars of vital consequence this bill embodies a radical departure from the traditional and long-established policy of this country, a policy in which our people have conceived the very character of their government to be expressed, the very mission and spirit of the nation in respect of its relations to the peoples of the world outside their borders. It seeks to all but close entirely the gates of asylum, which have always been open to those who could find nowhere else the right and opportunity of constitutional agitation for what they conceived to be the natural and inalienable rights of men, and it excludes those to

whom the opportunities of elementary education have been denied without regard to their
character, their purposes, or their natural
capacity."

The immigrant brings in a steady stream of
new life and new blood to the nation. The unskilled have made possible the construction of
great engineering works, have helped to build
bridges and roadways above and under ground.
The number of skilled artisans and craftsmen
 among immigrants and
the contribution they make
to the cultural side of our
national life are too rarely
emphasized. Alas for our
educational system! we
must still look abroad for
the expert cabinet-maker
or stone-carver, the weav-
er of tapestry, or the ar-
tistic worker in metals,
precious or base.

In another place I have spoken of the rise
of certain needle trades from those of sweaters
and sweaters' victims to a standardized industry, with an output estimated at hundreds of
millions yearly. The industry of cloak- and suit-
making has been to a large extent developed

by the immigrants themselves. When the stranger looks upon the loft buildings in other parts of the city, gigantic beehives with the swarms of workers going in and out, he seldom comprehends that great wealth has been created for the community by these humble workers.

The man who now stands at the gates of Ellis Island turns his socially trained mind toward the development of methods for the protection and assimilation of the immigrant after the gates have closed upon him. But the best conceived plans of this Commissioner of Immigration and others who have long studied the question will be fruitless unless, throughout the country, an intelligent and respectful attitude toward the stranger is sedulously cultivated.

In the early glow of our enthusiasm, when we were first brought in contact with the immigrant, we dreamed of making his coming of age—his admission to citizenship—something of a rite. Many who come here to escape persecution or the hardships suffered under a militaristic government idealize America. They bring an enthusiasm for our institutions that would make it natural to regard admission to the rights and responsibilities of citizenship with seriousness. Years ago we urged the use of school buildings, that registration and the casting of the ballot might be dignified by formal surroundings. This has been done in several cities, although not yet in New York.

The foreign press, particularly the Yiddish, has a distinct Americanizing influence. Many adults never learn the new language and, indeed, acquire here the habit of newspaper-reading. The history of the United States, biographies of George Washington, Abraham Lincoln, and other distinguished Americans appear in the pages of these papers, and one Italian daily published serially the Constitution of the United States. Effective, too, as an educational and assimilating measure have been the lectures in foreign languages conducted for many years by the Educational Alliance on East Broadway and by the various settlements, and included, for some years past, in the evening courses of the Department of Education.

In our neighborhood the physical changes of the last twenty years have been great. Since that first disturbing walk with the little girl to the rear tenement on Ludlow Street asphalt has replaced unclean, rough pavements; beautiful school buildings (some the finest in the world) have been erected; streets have been altered, and rows of houses demolished to make room for new bridges and small parks. Subway

AT ELLIS ISLAND
There is a stream of inflowing life

tubes take the working population to scattered parts of the greater city; piers have been built for recreation purposes, and a chain of small free libraries of beautiful design. A Tenement House Department has been created, charged with supervision and enforcement of the laws regulating the housing of 80 per cent. of the city's population, and so far assaults upon this protective legislation have been repulsed, despite the tireless lobby of the owners year after year.

As our neighbors have prospered many have moved to quarters where they find better houses, less congestion, more bathtubs; but an enormous working population still finds occupation in the lower part of the city. Carfare is an expense, and time spent in overcrowded cars, which scarcely afford standing-room, adds to the exhaustion of the long day, and these considerations keep many near the workshop. Despite the exodus, we still remain an overcrowded region of overcrowded homes. Through the tenements there is a stream of inflowing as well as outflowing life. The newcomer finds a lodging-place most readily in this vicinity, and the East Side is the shore of the harbor.

The settlements have been before the public long enough to have lost the glamour of moral adventure that was associated with their early days. Many who were identified with them then have steadfastly remained, although realizing, as one of them has said, that high purpose has often been mocked by petty achievement.

A characteristic service of the settlement to the public grows out of its opportunities for creating and informing public opinion. Its flexibility as an instrument makes it pliant to the essential demands made upon it; uncommitted to a fixed programme, it can move with the times.

Out of the enthusiasms and out of the sympathies of those who come to it, though they be sometimes crude and formless, a force is created that makes for progress. For these, as well as for the helpless and ignorant who seek aid and counsel, the settlement performs a function.

The visitors who come from all parts of the world and exchange views and experiences prove how absurd are frontiers between honest-thinking men and women of different nationalities or different classes. Human interest and passion for human progress break down barriers centuries old. They form a tie that binds closer than any conventional relationship.

INDEX

Adams, Maude, 87
Adolescence, problems of, and settlement work, 170-179, 189-199
Anarchism, 274-279
Archer, William, 272

Bellevue Hospital, 28, 59
Bialystok massacre, 230
Breshkovsky, Katharine, 238-248
Brewster, Mary, 8, 10, 16, 45, 48, 78, 113
Budget of a working-girl, 194; her "two jobs," 211

Cafés, bookshops, and saloons, 273-275
Child Hygiene, Bureau of, 53, 57, 59
Child labor:
  Children who work, 135-151; conditions in New York City, 135-137,—in Pennsylvania and the South, 144, 145; National Committee on, 144, 146; New York Committee on, 137, 144, 148, 150; newsboys, 146-149; obstacles to measures for protection of children, 149; scholarships to aid children, 138-142; statistics for Greater New York, 158; sweatshops and children, 153-156; typical employment record, 143; Washington Conference on, 146
Clubs and classes in the settlement, 179-184
Columbia University creates Department of Nursing and Health, 64
Committee of Fifteen (New York), inquiry of, 174

Comte, 274
Continuation Schools, necessary for young workers, 160
Convalescents, country house for, 88
Crosby, Ernest, 234, 235, 280

Davis, Katherine, 268
Defectives:
  Responsibility of society for, 122; special classes instituted, 117-120
De Leon, Daniel, 262
Diseases of children and home treatment, 38-40
Dock, L. L., 266
Doukhobors, the, 233-235
Drama:
  As a social force, 270-273; dramatic instinct of Jewish child, 184; marionette theater, 272; Neighborhood Playhouse, 185; pageants and plays, 184-187, 226; Yiddish plays, 270-272
Ducey, Father, 280
Dunsany, Lord, 188

Education:
  Bureau of vocational guidance proposed, 160; continuation schools necessary, 160; educational ideals and the settlement, 133; effects of disorganized tenement life on, 110-113; Federal Children's Bureau, 57, 163, 165, 166, 167, 168; foreign press as Americanizing influence, 307; hardships endured for, 99-103; institutional life and the child, 124-132; necessity for early care and training, 133; responsibility for defectives, 122; scholarships,

313